Evelyn Findlater's
WHOLEFOOD
Cookery Course

Evelyn Findlater's
WHOLEFOOD
Cookery Course

a Charles Herridge book
Frederick Muller   London

Published in Great Britain in 1984
by
Muller, Blond & White Ltd
55/57 Great Ormond Street
London WC1N 3HZ

Produced by Charles Herridge Ltd
Woodacott, Northam, Devon EX39 1NB
Photography by Jonathon Bosley
Drawings by Karen Baker
Printed in England by
Hazell Watson & Viney Ltd

ISBN 0 584 95065 9 (limp edition)
ISBN 0 584 95064 0 (cased edition)

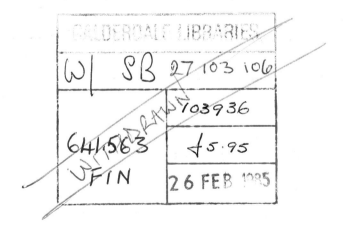

Contents

Introduction

This book is a course of cookery lessons and is the result of teaching many students the art of wholefood cookery. The classes were originally instigated by the customers in the wholefood shop and café my husband and I ran for three years in Devon. Much to their surprise, the food tasted delicious and I spent most of my time in the shop giving recipes and advice to keen and interested people who wished to change their existing diet to a healthier one.

The book is not just a conglomeration of healthy recipes but is designed to introduce wholefoods gradually into your daily diet in a way that is easy on the purse and on the digestion. I spent years trying out random recipes, which added strange ingredients to my store cupboard; some were successful to taste but played havoc with my digestion while others were downright disastrous. I won through in a hit and miss way. In devising my course I had to find an easier beginning that had a familiarity about it and would encourage people to succeed — producing not only healthy meals but also food that was deliciously acceptable to the palate. I also try to point out as simply as possible the nutritional value of the foods which, if gradually added to the diet in a balanced way, will help the body to function more efficiently within a very short time.

Through experience I have found that it is not a good idea to eat beans without the previous introduction of more easily digested wholefoods such as wholegrains. If this is not done, beans can cause in some people very unpleasant intestinal reactions. It is very important to educate the system slowly away from processed and less fibrous foods so that the body can adjust gradually to a very worthwhile and healthier way of eating without upset or disappointment.

Whether you eat meat or not, the addition of wholefoods and the elimination of refined and over-processed foods can only benefit your health. But I also believe that what we eat should taste really good and not just be good for us; it must be simple and delicious for every day, with added exotic flair for special occasions. This I have tried to fulfil in my book which, if followed lesson by lesson, will, I hope, open the doors to real enjoyment and healthier living.

Wholefoods are natural foods with, hopefully, nothing added to them, nothing taken away from them and free from harmful chemicals; these include such foods as 100% wholemeal flour, unpolished brown rice and other whole grains mentioned in the book, fresh fruit and vegetables (although these are hard to come by organically grown without sprays), dried peas and beans, dried fruit and all nuts and seeds. Meat, dairy produce and fish are also whole foods but it is only the few who can obtain these free range, where the animals have not been injected with hormones and the produce free from residual antibiotics.

A healthy diet is, of course, a question of balance whether you eat meat or not. The right amount of protein and unprocessed carbohydrates and an adequate supply of vitamins and minerals are essential to a fit and healthy body. We require a high intake of fibre and a low consumption of fats, sugar and salt. Research has shown that in our modern Western diet we lack sufficient fibre (roughage) and eat too much saturated fat, sugar and salt, added to which most of our refined foods contain chemicals.

As briefly as possible I will explain about fibre, fats, sugar and salt. Read about these before you start the lessons, although I have given information about the ingredients used in each lesson in separate introductions.

The Question of Fibre

First of all, a lack of fibre in your diet causes constipation which is a serious warning that the body is not functioning properly. Although fibre, which is found in plant cells, does not have any nutritional value and cannot be broken down by our digestive system, it absorbs water, becomes sponge-like and grips on to the muscles of the intestines. It thus helps to move whatever is in the digestive tract along more smoothly and eliminates it quickly from the body. Tests have shown that fibre can also absorb poisonous substances, dilute them and flush them out *daily*. It is not unusual for people who have low fibre diets to retain food residues for a week or more. Waste matter gets stuck in the intestinal tract. This can result in grave complications, one of which is diverticulitis, a swelling in the colon wall. Evidence shows that fibre can alter the bacteria in the bowel, making it less prone to disease. Dietary fibre is only present in vegetables, fruits and whole grain cereals.

PLANTS RICH IN FIBRE include apples, bananas, fresh blackberries, potatoes and all dried beans, peas and lentils. Grains rich in fibre include 100% wholemeal flour, brown, unpolished rice and oatmeal and, of course, all products made with these such as bread, cakes and biscuits.

Bran, which seems to be selling everywhere, is the fibrous part of the wholemeal grain, removed with the wheatgerm when white flour is produced. So it is advisable to add extra bran and wheatgerm to your diet if you use white flour regularly.

Fats — Which to Eat?

THE SATURATED FATS include animal fats, butter and cream, some margarines (unless otherwise stated), coconut and palm oils.

THE POLYUNSATURATED FATS include safflower seed oil (highest in linoleic acid which seems to play an important part in controlling cholesterol levels), sunflower oil, corn oil, wheatgerm oil, soya oil and vegetable margarines which state this on the label.

THE MONO-UNSATURATED FATS. Olive oil contains mono-unsaturated fatty acids which do not seem to contribute to heart disease. Although it is low in linoleic acid it has been found to increase the absorption of vitamins A, D, E and K and is completely digestible.

Findings have shown that if we eat *large amounts* of saturated fats we will produce too high a level of cholesterol in the blood and thus become more vulnerable to heart attacks, thrombosis and gallstones. Cholesterol is made by the body and is essential for certain functions. It is only when there is too much that problems arise.

On the other hand, unsaturated fats which are high in linoleic acid tend to lower the level of cholesterol in the blood. But it must also be mentioned that vitamins B and E are needed to maintain a low level of cholesterol.

Oils are either refined, semi-refined or cold pressed. The refined oils are often detergent-extracted and subjected to high temperatures to extract the oil quickly and cheaply. This removes valuable properties such as vitamins and minerals from the oil. In many cases chemicals are added. Semi-refined oil, where the extraction process is less intense, still contains some valuable nutrients. Cold pressed oil is whole and complete. It has simply been pressed slowly from the seeds, has a delicious taste and fresh smell and, although more expensive, I use it for all salad dressings and light sautéing. For deep frying the other oils mentioned will do as these are heated to a high temperature during cooking.

It would seem then that the most sensible course to take would be to replace saturated fats with unsaturated fats whenever possible and to cut down on bought cakes and biscuits, which are usually made with saturated fat and have a high sugar content. Cold pressed oils are definitely the best and a wise addition to your diet.

The Sugar Bug

Sugar is definitely not needed to give you energy. It supplies mostly calories. Other foods which do this will also give valuable nutrients — not so with sugar. Much evidence points to a connection between a high intake of pure sucrose (sugar) and diabetes.

There are, of course, minute amounts of minerals and vitamins in the naturally darker sugars (not dyed sugars) but these benefits are outweighed by the ill effects of eating sugar — tooth decay for a start. Don't panic, my recipes do contain sugar, but never white sugar. I do not feel fanatical about any foods because in sensible wholefood eating your body is more balanced and healthy and therefore well able to cope with a few indulgences. I try to use Barbados or molasses sugar as much as possible, as they do contain small amounts of vitamins, particularly of the B group, and minerals.

BLACKSTRAP MOLASSES is the residue left after sugar cane has been processed to produce pure white sugar (sucrose) and is a rich source of the B vitamins. It contains several more times the iron contained in the same amount of liver and more calcium than milk. Try to use this product instead of sugar whenever possible.

HONEY contains some vitamins and minerals but the main difference between honey and sugar is that it contains fructose or fruit sugar instead of sucrose. This fruit sugar is more easily assimilated by the body, but any sweet concentrates should be eaten in moderation and cut out whenever possible. Experiment with recipes by cutting down the amount of sugar required and you will find the results prove very successful. The less sugar you eat the less your body craves. Try to cut down gradually.

Salt — Why Cut it Down?

Evidence from health experts shows that heavy consumption of salt can lead to, among other ailments, arthritis and high blood pressure. It appears to overload the system with sodium and disturbs the balance with potassium. Again, like sugar, the less you eat the less you need. So try and cut down bit by bit and you will begin to taste the food rather than the salt.

All these nutritional facts and cautions point quite clearly to the importance of knowing more about the food we eat and why. Take care most of the time and moderate indulgences will be taken prompt care of by a balanced, healthy body.

LESSON 1

Breads and Yeast Recipes

SHOPPING LIST

Here is a short shopping list for Lesson 1 which will enable you to start a wholefood cupboard gradually. These ingredients will all be of use in other lessons in the book.

Wholemeal flour,
*   100% stoneground, plain*
Dried or fresh yeast
Jar of molasses
Jar of malt extract
Sesame seeds

Sea salt
Sunflower oil
Small bottle olive oil (cold pressed)
*   for pizza dough*
Soya flour
Rye flour

Which Flours to Use and Why

WHOLEMEAL FLOUR or 100% WHOLEMEAL contains all the bran and wheatgerm and is higher in nutritional value than any processed products from the whole grain. Stoneground wholemeal is best to use because the roller plates distribute the wheatgerm evenly throughout the flour. Steel plates, unfortunately, reach such a high speed that the heat produced can cause the wheatgerm to become rancid. Using steel plates is quicker and more economical but often produces an inferior flour.

85% or 81% EXTRACTION FLOUR (referred to as wheatmeal) has approximately 19 per cent of the ground grain removed. The wheatgerm and most of the bran is missing.

Wholemeal flour can be sieved and the bran retained to use in fillings so that the finished meal will still have the whole grain. For example, a lighter pastry will be achieved using sieved wholemeal flour. Save the bran, roll the pastry out in some of it and put the rest inside your fruit or savoury pies or flans.

UNBLEACHED WHITE FLOUR. I use this for sauces. About 35 per cent of the grain is removed. It is not good for general baking as there is no bran or wheatgerm left. Try to avoid using ordinary white flour, which is chemically treated and bleached by chlorine dioxide (also used for cleaning drains). Be wary of buying what is labelled brown bread as it is often bleached white bread with added colouring. This way the bread is still light in texture but brown in colour and popular demand for 'brown but light as a feather' keeps this inferior bread selling. To be on the safe side ask for 100 per cent wholemeal bread. Better still, make your own.

Opposite *(clockwise from top left)* Garlic French Loaf, Wholemeal Loaf, Pitta Breads, Pizza, Banana and Orange Peel Loaf (all recipes are in Lesson 1).

CRACKED KIBBLED WHEAT is whole wheat split by pressure machinery but still retaining its high nutritional value (see page 14 for a recipe using this wheat). It is really good sprinkled on top of bread or rolls before baking. Just egg the top lightly and trickle over a little kibbled wheat before baking.

RYE FLOUR has a distinctive flavour. It is slightly lower in gluten than wheat, which means it has less protein and the dough will not rise like wheat dough. A pure rye grain loaf will be heavier and flatter than bread made with wheat, but it has a delicious flavour and cuts very thinly. A good idea is to mix rye flour with wholemeal to achieve a different texture and flavour in your bread (see page 16). There are dark and light rye flours. The light variety contains less bran.

SOYA FLOUR. Although this flour is not from grain but from the soya bean I have included it in this lesson because I use it a great deal in bread making. It adds lots of protein, a lovely flavour and seems to lighten the dough, provided not too much is added. (See page 14 for a recipe using soya flour in bread making.) More notes on soya flour are on page 78.

BARLEY AND BARLEY FLOUR. Most barley flours are made from pearl barley, which is processed. *Pot barley* is the whole grain brown barley so use this in your soups and stews. (See page 120 for a hearty recipe.) I like to sprout the pot barley and use it in bread making. (See page 14 on sprouted grain bread.) It has a nutty, malty flavour. Two tablespoons of the grain, sprouted, will be sufficient. Follow instructions for wheat sprouts. If you can obtain the pot barley flour just add two cups to my basic bread recipe and take out two cups of wholemeal flour.

In breadmaking I often use malt, not just for its marvellous flavour but for its nutritional content as well. It is extracted from barley and moistens the dough so the liquid content must be adjusted accordingly.

I also use sesame seeds which are packed with vitamins, calcium, iron, protein and linoleic acid. More recipes using these precious seeds are given in the lesson on Nuts and Seeds.

Lots of you will have seen recipes for 'once only rising' breads. I have found that these often result in a heavier loaf. Two risings will lighten your bread considerably. Practice makes perfect. Make double lots and freeze some. It saves time. You can freeze some of the dough after the first kneading. When you want to use it just take it out and let it rise in the greased plastic bag overnight in a warm place. It will rise as it defrosts. Dough can also be left to rise overnight. Remember . . . only overheating the dough kills the yeast.

Basic Wholemeal Bread, Pitta Bread and Pizza Dough

This one dough will make all three recipes. The ingredients listed will make:

Two 1lb 4oz (560g) loaves, eight pitta breads and two pizzas 10in (25cm) in diameter or Four 1lb 4oz (560g) loaves or Thirty pitta breads, which can be frozen when cool, ready for quick, wholesome snacks.

You will need 1lb (450g) loaf tins, greased and floured for the bread, baking trays for the pitta breads (floured only) and two greased, 10in (25cm) ovenproof plates for the pizzas.

Set the oven to 450°F, 230°C, Gas Mark 8.

To make two loaves, eight pitta breads and two pizzas:

3·3 1lb (1·5kg) wholemeal, stoneground flour
1 level tablespoon (15ml) sea salt
4oz (110g) sesame seeds
just under 1¾ pints (1 litre) warm water
just over 1oz (30g) dried yeast or just under 2oz (50g) fresh yeast

approx 2 teaspoons (10ml) molasses
1 tablespoon (15ml) malt extract
2 tablespoons (30ml) corn or sunflower oil
a little beaten egg and 1 teaspoon sesame seeds for top of loaves

Mix the flour, salt and sesame seeds in a warm bowl and keep warm. Measure out the required warm water in a large jug. Take out ½ pint (275ml) to which you add the yeast and ¼ teaspoon of the molasses. Stir and leave to froth in a warm place for 5-7 minutes.

Add the malt extract, oil and 1 heaped teaspoon (9-10ml) molasses to the remaining warm water and stir.

When the yeast liquid is frothy add this, with the malted liquid, to the flour mixture by making a well in the middle and gradually working it into a soft dough. At this stage remember to leave some of the melted liquid in the jug so that you can be sure not to make the dough too wet. Flours differ in texture and absorb different amounts of liquid. Knead the dough for 7 minutes then place it in a greased polythene bag, leaving room for it to rise. Wrap in a warm towel and leave to rise for 45 minutes to 1 hour, then knock back and knead for 1 minute.

Your dough is now ready to use.

Cut the dough into four. Place two pieces back in the polythene bag and form the other two into loaves. Brush with beaten egg and sprinkle with sesame seeds. Place in the prepared loaf tins and leave to rise on top of the cooker for 20 minutes, covered with a damp cloth. Bake in the pre-heated oven, on the middle shelf at 450°F, 230°C, Gas Mark 8 for 10 minutes then at 375°F, 190°C, Gas Mark 5 for 25 minutes. Cool for 10 minutes in the tins then turn the bread out on to a wire rack.

To make eight pitta breads take out one of the two remaining pieces of dough, roll it into a long sausage and cut into 8 equal pieces. As you roll out each pitta, keep the little pieces just under the polythene bag. Use bran for rolling out to approximately 8in (20cm) long by 4in (10cm) centre width, forming an oval shape. Place each oval on to warmed, floured trays, covering them as you go with a damp cloth. They will look very thin but don't worry. Leave them to rise for 15-20 minutes then bake at 450°F, 230°C, Gas Mark 8 for 6 minutes only. You will need three trays — change the trays around in the oven after 3 minutes. The pittas will puff up in places. Don't touch them until they cool unless you want to fill them immediately. The pittas can be very slightly flattened and frozen if you make lots. To defrost, just pop in a warm oven for 3 minutes.

Try the Nutty Paté recipe on page 94 as a filling with salad or just slice open the pittas, spread a little margarine on both sides, place a generous amount of grated cheese and a little onion on one half and grill until lightly browned. Put bean sprouts and sliced red pepper on top of the cheese, replace the other half of the pitta and warm under the grill for a minute or two. A fabulous, wholesome meal in a moment.

Pizza

For this recipe you will need to add 2 tablespoons (30ml) olive oil to the remaining dough, to make two pizzas. Take out the last remaining dough and squash the olive oil into it. Mould it well for 2 minutes. Sprinkle bran on a board or worktop, cut the dough into two and roll out each piece to fit two 10in (25cm) greased ovenproof plates or pizza trays. Rolling out in bran crispens the dough. Leave to rise in a warm place, covered with a damp cloth, for about 20 minutes.

Set the oven to 375°F, 190°C, Gas Mark 5.

Filling for 2 pizzas

1 large onion, peeled and chopped
2 cloves garlic, peeled and chopped
a little oil for frying
½ red and ½ green pepper, de-seeded and chopped
4oz (110g) firm white mushrooms, washed and chopped
1 teaspoon (5ml) basil
1 teaspoon (5ml) oregano
2 bay leaves
½ teaspoon herb salt
freshly ground black pepper
2 tablespoons (30ml) tomato purée
1lb 12oz (794g) can tomatoes
8oz (225g) farmhouse Cheddar cheese, grated
12 black olives, halved

Sauté the onion and garlic in a little oil for 10 minutes, add the chopped peppers and mushrooms and sauté for a further 3 minutes. Add the herbs, salt, pepper, tomato purée and tomatoes. Simmer for 30 minutes. Spread on the pizzas. Sprinkle with the grated cheese and decorate with the olives and a little oregano. Bake in the pre-heated oven for 30 minutes. Let the pizza set for 10 minutes before cutting.

Bread with a Different Flavour

Once you have mastered the basic wholemeal loaf it is very easy to vary the flavour and texture by adding different flours, fruits and seeds. Here are just a few for you to try.

Sprouted Grain Bread

Just add 2 cups of sprouted wheat to the basic dough ingredients and omit the sesame seeds. Mix the sprouted grain with the flour before adding the liquid. See page 108 on sprouting beans, seeds and grains.

Kibbled Wheat Loaf

Omit the sesame seeds from the basic recipe. Take out 2 cups of wholemeal flour and add 2 cups of kibbled or crushed wheat. Soak the crushed wheat in the required amount of warm liquid for 1 hour before making the bread.

Soya Flour and Wholemeal Bread

Opposite (right) Pitta Breads with salad filling, (left) Hummous (see page 128).

By adding soya flour you add more protein and lighten your bread. Take out 2 cups of the wholemeal flour and add 2 cups of soya flour to the basic recipe.

Rye Flour and Wholemeal Bread (with caraway seeds)

Do exactly as for soya flour and wholemeal bread. Add 4 teaspoons (20ml) caraway seeds to the flour.

Banana and Orange Peel Loaf

Leave out the malt extract and sesame seeds and use half and half 100% wholemeal flour and unbleached white flour. Add 4 mashed bananas, 4 beaten eggs and the grated rinds of 4 oranges to the liquid of the basic wholemeal bread recipe. You will, of course, need a little less liquid. Make sure that the liquid level is still *just* under 1¾ pints (1 litre) after adding the eggs, peel and mashed bananas. This recipe is truly delicious for a special tea time.

Garlic French Loaves

Makes 6.

Very suitable for freezing. No malt needed. This dough is very light in texture. Again referring to the basic recipe, take out 5 cups of wholemeal and add 2 cups of soya flour and 3 cups of *unbleached* white flour. Add 1 beaten egg and 12 good size cloves of garlic, crushed, to the liquid. Remember that the liquid must be just under 1¾ pints (1 litre) including the egg and garlic. After the first rising knead the dough for a few minutes then cut into twelve pieces. Keep the pieces in a plastic bag while you roll out each one into a snake shape 12in (30cm) long and 1½in (4cm) in diameter. Three will fit on to an average, floured, baking tray. Gently score the tops with seven strokes. Allow to rise for 30 minutes in a warm place, covered with a damp cloth, and bake in a hot oven 450°F, 230°C, Gas Mark 8, for 15 minutes.

If you do not want to make quite so many French loaves all at once you can make this mixture up into two standard loaves and three French loaves. Omit the garlic from the recipe and add it to the butter or polyunsaturated margarine when serving the hot French bread. One crushed clove of garlic per 2oz (50g) butter or margarine, blended together well, is sufficient.

Good luck with these delicious breads. Consult the index for any ingredients in the lesson which are not familiar to you.

All that remains is to get cracking on Lesson 1 and those you feed, including yourself, will be enriched by good, healthy food with a fabulous taste.

Pastry, Savoury and Sweet

LESSON 2

SHOPPING LIST

Some of the items needed are already listed in Lesson 1 so I will not include them here. I have omitted fresh vegetables from the list as you will be quite familiar with them.

Wholemeal flour, 100%
  stoneground, self-raising
Barbados sugar
Fruit sugar
Polyunsaturated margarine
Dried skimmed milk powder
  (no additives)
Shoyu (naturally fermented
  soy sauce)
Flageolet beans (haricot will do)
85% (wheatmeal) flour for
  thickening or sauces
Vegetable stock cubes (the 'with
  salt' kind)
Aduki beans
Dried apricots
Figs
Dates
Raisins
Apple juice concentrate
Honey

Pumpkin seeds
Almonds
Hazel-nuts
Cashews
Sunflower seeds

Herbs
Mixed herbs
Oregano
Tarragon
Aniseed (not star anise)
Fresh parsley
Herb salt

Spices
Black peppercorns
Mustard powder
Mace
Cinnamon
Clove powder
Nutmeg

Forget all those stories about heavy wholemeal pastry and have a go at these recipes which have been tried out with great success on the most hardened white pastry addicts. This lesson includes quiches (flans), pies, pastries and sweet pastry dishes.

The basic pastry recipes are given below and it is a good idea to make three or four times the quantity at once and freeze what you don't immediately need, ready for rolling and filling for a quick meal or a sweet dish. I have also included sweet and savoury crumble mixtures which can be frozen and sprinkled on the filling while still frozen — just take care not to squash the crumble together when freezing.

Basic Never-Fail Wholemeal Savoury Pastry

*Sufficient to make one
10in (25cm) quiche case.*

4oz (110g) polyunsaturated
   margarine
3 tablespoons (45ml) cold
   water
4oz (110g) wholemeal flour,
   plain (strong is best)

4oz (110g) wholemeal flour,
   self-raising
good pinch of salt

Mix the flours together. Put the margarine, water and 2 tablespoons (30ml) of the flour into a mixing bowl and cream for 1 minute. Gradually add the rest of the flour and the salt. Mix well together with the hands to form a soft, firm dough. Knead for 1 minute. Put the dough into a plastic bag and refrigerate for 30 minutes. Flour the table and rolling pin and roll out the pastry. Lift the pastry from the table with a palette knife, ease it over the rolling pin and place carefully into the greased flan dish or tin. Either freeze for 15 minutes or put in the fridge for 30 minutes. Now it is ready to bake blind and fill.

Basic Wholemeal Cheese Pastry

Make exactly as the wholemeal pastry. Stir in 2oz (50g) of grated Cheddar cheese after creaming the margarine, water and flour, and before adding the remaining flour.

Basic Wholemeal Sweet Pastry

To the basic wholemeal savoury recipe just add 1 rounded dessertspoon (20ml) of dark soft cane sugar or 1 rounded teaspoon (10ml) of fruit sugar. Or add 3 tablespoons (45ml) of cold apple juice instead of the cold water. For an extra light sweet pastry, sieve the wholemeal flour, save the bran and sprinkle it on the greased dish or tin before laying the pastry on to it. I prefer this method for sweet flans. An even lighter mixture is obtained by using one egg yolk and 2 tablespoons (30ml) of cold water for the liquid.

Sweet Crumble Mix

8oz (225g) wholemeal flour,
   plain
4oz (110g) polyunsaturated
   margarine
2 tablespoons (30ml) sesame
   seeds

2 tablespoons (30ml) dark soft
   cane sugar (optional)
good pinch salt
1 teaspoon (5ml) cinnamon
¼ teaspoon clove powder

Mix all the ingredients together to a rough breadcrumb mixture and press gently over the fruit. Soaked dried apricots with a little honey and grated raw apple are delicious.

Savoury Crumble Mix

As an easy alternative to rolling out pastry for vegetable pies here is a really tasty savoury topping.

8oz (225g) wholemeal flour, plain
4oz (110g) polyunsaturated margarine

2oz (50g) farmhouse Cheddar cheese, grated
good pinch sea salt

Mix all to a crumb-like mixture and spread over the vegetables and sauce.

Cake-Like Wholemeal Pastry

This is a light, spongy, cake-like pastry.

10oz (275g) polyunsaturated margarine
3oz (75g) soft light muscovado sugar
2 egg yolks
2 tablespoons (30ml) cold water

8oz (225g) 100% wheatmeal flour, plain
8oz (225g) 81% wheatmeal flour, self-raising
pinch sea salt

Cream the margarine and the sugar for a couple of minutes. Whisk the egg yolks with the water until frothy then pour into the margarine and sugar mixture. Mix the two flours and the salt together, add 4 tablespoons (60ml) to the creamed mixture and continue creaming, gradually adding the rest of the flour. Mould into a soft dough and knead for 1 minute then put into a plastic bag and chill in the fridge for 30 minutes or in the freezer for 10 minutes. The dough will roll out easily if you sprinkle flour on the surface and place a clear plastic sheet on top to roll out.

Quiches, Pies and Pasties

Tomato, Mushroom and Onion Quiche

Make a 10in (25cm) pastry case with the basic savoury pastry, prick the base and bake blind at 375°F, 190°C, Gas Mark 5, for 10 minutes. Leave to cool.

Filling

4 large eggs, separated
6fl oz (175ml) milk
1 tablespoon (15ml) dried milk powder
2 tablespoons (30ml) thick yoghurt (see page 130)
½ teaspoon ground mace
½ teaspoon sea salt
freshly ground black pepper
5oz (150g) farmhouse Cheddar cheese, grated
1 small onion, peeled and thinly sliced in rings
2 medium tomatoes, cut into 8 slices
6 button mushrooms, sliced
1 teaspoon (5ml) oregano

Whisk the egg whites, add the yolks, milk, milk powder, yoghurt, mace, sea salt and black pepper. Whisk all well together. Sprinkle 2oz (50g) of the grated cheese in the base of the cooked quiche case and spread the onion rings thinly over this. Cover with more cheese, leaving just a little for the top of the quiche. Place the tomatoes 1in (2·5cm) from the edge of the quiche. Dot with the mushrooms. Pour the egg mixture over this and finally sprinkle the remaining grated cheese and the oregano over the top. Bake in the centre of the oven for 40 minutes at 375°F, 190°C, Gas Mark 5.

Asparagus Quiche with Tarragon *(illustrated on page 23)*

Prepare a 10in (25cm) pastry case as directed in the recipe for Tomato, Mushroom and Onion Quiche.

Filling

6oz (175g) asparagus spears (8 spears)
1 very small onion, peeled and very finely chopped
5oz (150g) farmhouse Cheddar cheese, grated
4 large eggs, separated
1 tablespoon (15ml) thick cream
2 tablespoons (30ml) thick yoghurt (see page 130)
6fl oz (175ml) milk
½ teaspoon mace
freshly ground black pepper
½ teaspoon sea salt
½ teaspoon dried tarragon

If the asparagus is frozen, steam for 10 minutes. If fresh, cut off the hard, woody ends and steam for 20 minutes or boil in slightly salted water for 12 minutes. Chop approximately 1in (2·5cm) off the bottom of each spear. Then chop these pieces in half. You will then have sixteen little pieces plus eight good size spears. Spread the onion and the ½in (1cm) pieces of asparagus all round the base of the cooked pastry case. Cover with most of the cheese, leaving just a little for the top. Whisk the egg whites for 1 minute, add the yolks, cream, yoghurt, milk, mace, pepper and sea salt. Pour over the cheese. Place the eight spears, with the tips 1in (2·5cm) from the edge, all round the quiche. Sprinkle with the remaining cheese and the tarragon. Bake for 40 minutes in the centre of the oven at 375°F, 190°C, Gas Mark 5. Serve hot or, even better, cold — delicious and very special.

Spinach, Cottage Cheese and Yoghurt Quiche

Prepare a 10in (25cm) pastry case as directed in the recipe for Tomato, Mushroom and Onion Quiche.

Filling

4 large eggs, separated
8oz (225g) cottage cheese
8oz (225g) frozen or fresh spinach, cooked
2oz (50g) strong Cheddar cheese, grated
4 tablespoons thick yoghurt (see page 130)

1 tablespoon (15ml) thick cream (optional)
½ teaspoon sea salt
½ teaspoon mace
1 good size clove garlic, crushed
freshly ground black pepper

Whisk the egg whites for 1 minute, add the yolks and whisk well in. Add the cottage cheese. Add the spinach after squeezing all the liquid out of it. (Save the liquid for gravy or soup.) Fork in all the other ingredients. Pour into the cooked pastry case and bake for 40 minutes in centre of the oven at 375°F, 190°C, Gas Mark 5. Superb served with jacket potatoes and Orange, Tomato and Onion Salad (see page 113).

Giant Vegetable Pasty

You will need double the basic savoury pastry mixture (see page 18). When making this pastry you can use 3oz (75g) cream cheese and 3oz (75g) margarine to 8oz (225g) of flour to make a truly light and special pastry.

Set the oven to 375°F, 190°C, Gas Mark 5.

Serves 6.

Filling

4 tablespoons (60ml) sunflower or olive oil
1 large onion, peeled and chopped
4 small new potatoes or 2 medium old potatoes, scrubbed, diced into ¾in (2cm) cubes and steamed for 10 minutes
2 medium carrots, scrubbed and thinly sliced
2 courgettes, washed and sliced
2 sticks celery, chopped
2 cloves garlic, crushed
4oz (110g) button mushrooms, washed and sliced (optional)
1 small green pepper, de-seeded and chopped

1 teaspoon (5ml) mixed herbs
1 tablespoon (15ml) fresh parsley, chopped
freshly ground black pepper
1 cup flageolet or haricot beans, cooked (see page 60 on cooking beans)
1 tablespoon (15ml) wholemeal flour, plain
5 medium tomatoes, skinned and chopped
1 tablespoon (15ml) tomato purée
1 vegetable stock cube
beaten egg to glaze

Sauté the onion, potato and carrot for 10 minutes. Add the courgettes, celery and garlic. Sauté for 5 minutes. Add the mushrooms, green pepper, herbs, parsley, pepper and beans. Sauté for 3 minutes. Stir in the flour and continue sautéing for just one minute. Finally add the tomatoes, mixed with the tomato purée and stock cube before stirring in. You will end up with a slightly moist but not too wet mixture. Let it get cold. Roll out the pastry on a large sheet of greaseproof paper, to a circle about 18in (46cm) in diameter. On one half of the circle place the cold, cooked vegetable mixture (save any excess juice for gravy) and lift the other half over the top with the aid of the greaseproof paper it is resting on. Smear the edges with beaten egg and press firmly together. Cut out pastry leaves to decorate. Glaze the top with beaten egg. Place the giant pasty and its greaseproof paper base on a greased baking tray and bake for 30 minutes in centre of the oven.

This can also be made into six or eight individual size pasties which are much more manageable to prepare and delicious hot or cold. You can also use other beans in this recipe — soya or red kidney beans go well.

Leek and Potato Pie *(illustrated opposite)*

I like the pastry on top of this pie to be quite thick, so I use one and a half times the basic savoury or cheese pastry mix (see page 18). Have the pastry ready to roll out. This quantity is enough for an 8 x 12in (20 x 30cm) pie dish.

Set the oven to 375°F, 190°C, Gas Mark 5.

Serves 6.

Filling
3 good size potatoes scrubbed and chopped into ½in (1cm) cubes
1 teaspoon (5ml) herb salt to boil potatoes (makes good stock)
4 good size leeks, washed and chopped into 1in (2.5cm) pieces, leaving as much green on as possible
3 sticks celery, chopped
1¼ pints (750ml) mixed milk and stock (from boiling potatoes)
2 tablespoons (30ml) polyunsaturated margarine
2 tablespoons (30ml) 81% (wheatmeal) flour, plain
½ teaspoon dry mustard powder
4oz (110g) farmhouse Cheddar cheese, grated
1 tablespoon (15ml) fresh parsley, chopped
sea salt
freshly ground black pepper
a little beaten egg to glaze

Boil the potatoes in a little water seasoned with herb salt for 4 minutes. Add the leeks and celery and simmer for another 3 minutes. The vegetables should still be firm. Drain, saving the water. Place the vegetables in a greased pie dish. Add enough warm milk to the cooking water to make up to 1¼ pints (750ml) of liquid in all and keep it warm. Melt the margarine in a dry, thick saucepan. Take off the heat and stir in the flour and mustard powder with a wooden spoon. Gradually add the warm liquid, stirring constantly. Return the pan to the heat, bring to the boil and simmer for 3 minutes, stirring all the time until thick and smooth. Take off the heat. Add the grated cheese, parsley, salt and pepper to taste. The sauce will still be quite runny. Pour the sauce over the vegetables and leave to cool for 15 minutes. Roll out the pastry thickly to fit over the vegetables and sauce. Glaze the top with the beaten egg and bake in the centre of the pre-heated oven for 30 minutes.

Serve with a little mustard and fresh green salad.

Opposite *(left)* Asparagus Quiche with Tarragon (see page 20) *(right)* Leek and Potato Pie.

Aduki Bean Pie

You will need a 10in (25cm) greased dish plus one and a half times the basic savoury or cheese pastry mix (see page 18). Divide the pastry in half and line the pie dish with one half. Prick the base. Bake for 10 minutes at 375°F, 190°C, Gas Mark 5, then leave to cool. Save the other half of the pastry for the top of the pie.

Serves 6.

Filling

just over 8oz (250g) aduki beans, soaked and cooked (see page 57)
4 tablespoons (60ml) sunflower or olive oil
1 large onion, peeled and chopped
1 clove garlic, crushed
2 sticks celery, chopped
4oz (110g) button mushrooms, sliced (optional)

2 tablespoons (30ml) fresh parsley, chopped
14oz (396g) can tomatoes
freshly ground black pepper
1 tablespoon (15ml) shoyu (naturally fermented soy sauce)

The beans will have soaked up most of the liquid when cooking. If not, drain them. Sauté the onion, garlic and celery for 5 minutes, then add the mushrooms and parsley and continue to sauté for 3 minutes. Mix the beans with the tomatoes, sautéd vegetables, pepper and shoyu. Simmer for 5 minutes. Leave to cool for 20 minutes then pour into the cooked pie case. Roll out the other half of the pastry and with the aid of the rolling pin, put on top of the aduki filling. Crimp the edges. Prick the top and bake for 40 minutes at 375°F, 190°C, Gas Mark 5. Serve with mustard. Lovely with cooked green vegetables or green salad.

For a quick pie just put the filling in the baking dish and cover with the Savoury Crumble Mix (see page 19). Really easy and tastes lovely.

Sweet Pastry Delights

Soft Fruit Flan

For this recipe you will need a 9in (22cm) loose-bottomed flan tin. Line it with basic wholemeal sweet pastry or cake-like wholemeal pastry (quantities as ingredients on pages 18 and 19). The cake-like pastry might break when rolling out but just 'patchwork' it on to the well-greased tin.

Bake blind for 10 minutes at 400°F, 200°C, Gas Mark 6. Leave to cool before filling.

Filling

1lb (450g) soft fruit (e.g. raspberries, strawberries, etc.)
½ pint (275ml) water
2 tablespoons (30ml) apple juice concentrate

2 tablespoons (30ml) soft light muscovado sugar
2 teaspoons (10ml) arrowroot

Put the water, apple juice concentrate and sugar into a saucepan and heat, stirring constantly until the sugar has dissolved. Remove from the heat and put the fruit into the hot syrup. Leave for 3 minutes then strain off the liquid through a sieve. Mix the arrowroot with a little of the syrup, pour the rest of the syrup back into the saucepan, stir in the arrowroot mixture and bring to the boil, stirring all the time until it thickens. Leave to cool but do not allow to set. Arrange the fruit in the pastry case, spread the thickened syrup over this and leave to set. Serve with whipped cream.

Simple Apple Pie

You will need an 8-9in (20-23cm) pie dish approximately 2in (5cm) deep.

Set the oven to 400°F, 200°C, Gas Mark 6.

3 large, green cooking apples, cored and thinly sliced (leave skins on)
4 tablespoons (60ml) dark soft brown sugar
½ teaspoon cinnamon
¼ teaspoon nutmeg
¼ teaspoon ground cloves

1oz (30g) polyunsaturated margarine
basic wholemeal sweet pastry (quantity as the recipe on page 18)
1 dessertspoon (10ml) fruit sugar

Place the apple slices with the brown sugar and spices in layers in the greased pie dish. Dot with the margarine, cover with foil and bake for 15-20 minutes until apples are fairly soft. Leave to cool. Roll out the pastry to a 10in (25cm) circle and place on top of the apples. Turn in the edges and mark with a fork or crimp with the fingers. Brush the top lightly with cold water and sprinkle the fruit sugar over this. Fruit sugar is white and will give a crisp top to the pastry. Bake for 25-30 minutes. Best served hot.

Apple Meringue Pie

This recipe is a nice change from the traditional lemon meringue pie and it has a delicious flavour. You will require an 8in (20cm) pie dish. Line the base with my basic sweet pastry, using only 6oz (175g) flour instead of 8oz (225g). Adjust the quantities of the other ingredients accordingly. Prick the pastry and bake blind for 10 minutes at 375°F, 190°C, Gas Mark 5. Set aside to cool.

Filling
2 large cooking apples, peeled thinly and chopped
juice and grated rind of 1 small lemon
2oz (50g) fruit sugar
½ teaspoon cinnamon

¼ teaspoon clove powder

Meringue topping
2 eggs
2oz (50g) fruit sugar or **soft light sugar**

Cook the apples with the lemon juice and rind, 2oz (50g) fruit sugar and the spices until a pulp. Cool slightly. Separate the eggs and beat the egg yolks into the fruit mixture. Spoon into the prepared pastry case. To make the meringue topping, whisk the egg whites until stiff then gradually beat in the sugar. Spread this over the fruit pulp. Bake for 25 minutes at 325°F, 160°C, Gas Mark 3 if you wish to serve the pie hot, or for 1 hour at 275°F, 140°C, Gas Mark 1 if you wish to serve it cold. The slower method will produce a crisper meringue.

To vary this recipe you can use dried apricots with the apple. In this case, soak 2oz (50g) dried apricots and cook these with one large cooking apple instead of the two given in the basic recipe.

Fig and Aniseed Slice

You will need one baking tray approximately 8 x 12in (20 x 30cm) and 1½in (4cm) deep.

Set the oven to 375°F, 190°C, Gas Mark 3.

1lb (450g) dried figs
½ pint (275ml) water
3 teaspoons (15ml) aniseed (not star anise)

cake-like wholemeal pastry mixture (see page 19) made with
1lb (450g) flour
a little beaten egg to glase

Cut the stalks off the figs. Chop the figs as small as possible and simmer with the water and aniseed until the fruit is pulp-like. Cool. Chill the pastry for 30 minutes before use. Cut the pastry in half and roll out one half to fit the base of the tin, placing a sheet of plastic over the pastry when rolling out to make the job easier. You might have to 'patchwork' the pastry a little into the tin but it will smooth out in cooking. Prick the pastry base and bake blind for 10 minutes in the pre-heated oven. Spread the filling over the pastry base, roll out the remaining pastry and place over the filling. Brush a little egg over the pastry and bake for 45 minutes to 1 hour.

Date and Apple Slice *(illustrated opposite)*

This is a variation of the previous recipe. The only difference is the filling.

Opposite *(top)* Date and Apple Slice, *(bottom)* Apricot, Almond and Apple Flan (see page 150).

Filling
1lb (450g) dates, chopped
1lb (450g) green cooking apples, peeled, cored and chopped
½ teaspoon clove powder

1 teaspoon (5ml) ground cinnamon
¼ pint (150ml) water

Just simmer all the ingredients in a saucepan until the fruit is soft and mushy. Cool and use to fill the slice.

Cakes and Biscuits

LESSON 3

SHOPPING LIST

By now you should have a reasonable wholefood store cupboard. I will only add those ingredients not already listed in the first two lessons. I have left out the special luxury Christmas Cake and Pudding recipe ingredients.

Pecan nuts (hazel-nuts will do)
Walnuts
Currants
Sultanas
Glacé cherries
Dried apples
Desiccated coconut
Cream cheese (Philadelphia is best)
Vanilla essence

Carob powder or *flour*
Demerara sugar
Malt extract
Porridge oats
Molasses

Spices
Allspice
Ground ginger
Fresh ginger

There are lots more ingredients in this lesson but most you will probably have already.

The following recipes I hope will prove to you, once and for all, that cakes can be light and scrumptious using wholemeal flour.

After being in our shop for six months, slaving away in the kitchen from six in the morning, in walked Carol who said, 'Do you need anyone who can bake cakes?' In desperation I gave her a bunch of recipes and said, 'Add anything you like to this list so long as it is wholefoods.' I piled her trolley with the ingredients and off she went. She arrived back two days later with cakes that looked alive and tasted just beautiful. I owe her such a great deal. Wholefoods were quite new to her at the time and I think she was nervous of using them. From that very first day all we needed to discuss was an idea and the results were invariably delicious. Try these recipes and I am sure they will be thoroughly enjoyed and simple to make. There is a marvellous cheesecake recipe and at the end of this lesson I have included some popular Christmas recipes.

These recipes are designed to set you off in cake making using wholesome ingredients, but experiment for yourself and you will find that if you stick to the basic recipe you can substitute with great success. For instance, note that the carrot cake has oil instead of margarine. I have tried Carol's Devonshire Apple and Sultana Cake (page 30) using 8fl oz (225ml) sunflower oil instead of margarine and the result was just as good.

Note that I have used carob powder or flour instead of chocolate or cocoa powder because it is caffeine free, not bitter, naturally sweet and much cheaper. The bean is from the locust tree and is an ingredient in many Middle Eastern delicacies. Another reason for using this product instead of chocolate is that cocoa beans are high in oxalic acid which is known to 'lock in' calcium and thus make it unavailable to the body. So have a go with carob powder or flour. Fruit sugar is sweeter than cane sugar so when using this I use one third less of the required amount of sugar. It is good to use in cheesecake recipes as it is white in colour. Just remember that cakes should be a special treat occasionally, not a daily necessity.

Cakes

Carrot and Pecan Nut Cake

Hazel-nuts are a good substitute if you can't get pecan nuts. You will need a 10in (25cm) round or square, loose-bottomed cake tin or a 2lb (900g) loaf tin, greased and lined.

Set the oven to 325°F, 160°C, Gas Mark 3.

12fl oz (350ml) corn or **sunflower oil**
8oz (225g) Barbados sugar
1 flat teaspoon (5ml) clove powder
good pinch sea salt (optional)
4 large eggs, separated
12oz (350g) wholemeal flour, self-raising

1lb (450g) carrots, peeled and finely grated
4oz (110g) pecan nuts or **hazel-nuts, chopped**

Filling (optional)
4oz (110g) cream cheese
1 flat dessertspoon (10ml) clear honey

With a wooden spoon, beat the oil with the sugar for 1 minute, add the clove powder and salt. Whisk the egg whites for 1 minute and then the egg yolks for 1 minute. Add the whites to the oil mixture, then the yolks. Gradually fold in the flour. Finally fork in the carrots and chopped nuts. Spoon into the prepared tin and bake for 2 hours in the centre of the oven. (Allow 2½ hours if using the loaf tin.) The cake is delicious on its own, with fresh cream, or slice in half and fill with the cream cheese and honey mixed together. If you wish you can divide the mixture in two, place into 1lb (450g) loaf tins and bake for 1½ hours.

Banana and Walnut Cake

You will need a 10in (25cm) round or square cake tin, greased and lined.

Set the oven to 325°F, 160°C, Gas Mark 3.

8oz (225g) polyunsaturated margarine
8oz (225g) Barbados or soft dark sugar
pinch sea salt
4 large eggs, separated

12oz (350g) wholemeal flour, self-raising
1lb (450g) ripe bananas, mashed
4oz (110g) walnuts, roughly chopped

Cream the margarine and sugar for 3 minutes only and add the salt. Beat the egg whites for 1 minute. Beat the yolks for 1 minute. Add the egg whites to the margarine and sugar, then add the yolks. Gradually fold in the flour. Finally stir in the mashed bananas and nuts. Spoon into the tin and bake for 2 hours in the centre of the oven.

Carol's Devonshire Apple and Sultana Cake *(illustrated opposite)*

You will need a 10in (25cm) round or square cake tin, greased and lined.

Set the oven to 350°F, 180°C, Gas Mark 4.

12oz (350g) wholemeal flour, self-raising
¼ teaspoon clove powder
½ teaspoon cinnamon
8oz (225g) polyunsaturated margarine

8oz (225g) Barbados sugar
6oz (175g) sultanas
1lb (450g) cooking apples, thinly peeled, cored and diced
4 eggs, separated

Put the flour and spices in a bowl. Rub in the margarine until the mixture looks like crumbs. Stir in the sugar, sultanas and diced apples. Beat the egg whites for 1 minute. Beat the egg yolks for 1 minute. Stir both into the cake mixture with a fork so that you do not squash the apples. The mixture will not seem wet enough but it will become moist as the apples cook. Place in the tin and bake for 1¾-2 hours. Dredge the top with soft dark sugar mixed with a little cinnamon while the cake is still hot.

Coconut, Orange and Lemon Cake

You will need an 8in (20cm) cake tin, greased and lined.

Set the oven to 375°F, 190°C, Gas Mark 5.

Opposite *(top right)* Wholemeal Shortbread and Carob Shortbread (see page 41), *(bottom left)* Carol's Devonshire Apple and Sultana Cake.

8oz (225g) polyunsaturated margarine
8oz (225g) dark brown sugar
4 eggs, separated
8oz (225g) wholemeal flour, self-raising

6oz (175g) desiccated coconut
juice and rind of ½ lemon
juice and rind of ½ orange

Cream the margarine and sugar for 3 minutes. Add the beaten egg whites, then add the beaten yolks. Fold in the flour and coconut. Finally add the juice and grated rinds of the fruit. Bake in the centre of the oven for 45 minutes.

Spicy Fruit Cake

The variety of fruits and spices used in this recipe really give the cake an extra special flavour. The ingredients listed will make 1 large 3lb (1·5kg) cake or two smaller cakes weighing approximately 1½lb (750g) each.

Set the oven to 325°F, 160°C, Gas Mark 3.

8oz (225g) polyunsaturated margarine
8oz (225g) Barbados sugar
4 eggs, beaten
1 level teaspoon (5ml) nutmeg
¼ teaspoon cloves
½ teaspoon allspice
12oz (350g) wholemeal flour, self-raising

grated rind of ½ lemon
grated rind of ½ orange
2oz (50g) each raisins, currants, sultanas, glacé cherries, chopped dried apricots, chopped dried apple (a total of 12oz (350g) in all)

Cream the margarine and sugar for 3 minutes only and add the beaten eggs gradually. Mix the spices with the flour and fold into the mixture. Add the orange and lemon rinds and stir in the dried fruit. Place in the greased and lined tin or tins.

If making one large cake bake for 2¼-2½ hours. If making two smaller cakes bake for 1½ hours in the centre of the oven.

Apricot and Cinnamon Cake *(illustrated on page 39)*

You will need an 8in (20cm) round cake tin, greased and lined.

Set the oven to 325°F, 160°C, Gas Mark 3.

6oz (175g) polyunsaturated margarine
4½oz (125g) Barbados sugar
2 good tablespoons (45ml) clear honey
2 rounded teaspoons (10ml) cinnamon

3 eggs, beaten
10oz (275g) wholemeal flour, self-raising
2 tablespoons (30ml) milk
6oz (175g) dried apricots, washed and thoroughly dried

Cream the margarine and sugar for 3 minutes. Mix the honey and cream well in. Stir in the cinnamon. Add the beaten eggs, fold in the flour, add the milk and finally the chopped apricots. Pour into the prepared tin and bake for 1½ hours.

It is important to clean and dry the apricots because they might sink to the bottom of the cake if used when they are still wet.

Carob Cake

See the introduction to cake making, which tells you more about carob flour or powder. This is a very large, rich cake to be cut in small slices only. You will need a 10in (25cm) square or round cake tin, greased and lined.

Set the oven to 325°F, 160°C, Gas Mark 3.

10oz (275g) Barbados sugar
10oz (275g) polyunsaturated margarine
5 eggs, beaten
2 rounded tablespoons (40ml) carob flour mixed with enough water to make a smooth cream
10oz (275g) wholemeal flour, self-raising

Topping
4fl oz (120ml) double cream, whipped
2oz (50g) melted carob bar
1oz (25g) flaked almonds, toasted

Best results are in a mixer, but it is not essential. Cream the sugar and margarine for 5 minutes until smooth and light. Add the beaten eggs as slowly as possible. If using a liquidiser add the eggs a dessertspoonful at a time. It's a bother, but lightens the cake considerably. Fold in the carob mixture then gradually fold in the flour. Put the mixture into the prepared tin and bake for 1 hour. When cool, spread with the whipped cream to which you have added the melted carob bar. Top with the toasted flaked almonds. To make toasted flaked almonds, put them on a tray on a low shelf in the oven for 10 minutes while the cake is cooking.

Ginger and Honey Cake

Moist and deliciously gingery, just as it should be. You will require an 8in (20cm) round cake tin, greased and lined.

Set the oven to 325°F, 160°C, Gas Mark 3.

12oz (350g) wholemeal flour, self-raising
1 heaped teaspoon (10ml) mixed spice
1 heaped teaspoon (10ml) ground ginger
2oz (50g) fresh ginger, grated

5oz (150g) polyunsaturated margarine
7fl oz (200ml) clear honey
5oz (150g) demerara sugar
3 eggs, beaten
2 tablespoons (30ml) milk

Mix the flour with the spices and fresh ginger. Melt the margarine, honey and sugar (do not boil). Pour into the dry ingredients and mix well. Add the beaten eggs. Finally add the milk and mix in well. Place in the prepared tin and bake for 1½ hours.

Nicola's Victoria Sandwich

The best results, for a really light sponge, will be achieved if you have an electric mixer. You will need two 9in (23cm) sandwich tins, greased.

Set the oven to 375°F, 190°C, Gas Mark 5.

6oz (175g) polyunsaturated margarine
6oz (175g) demerara or soft dark sugar

3 eggs, beaten
6oz (175g) wholemeal or 81% (wheatmeal) flour, self-raising
2 drops vanilla essence

(A tip from Nicola who makes these to perfection. Weigh the eggs in their shells and then add the exact weight of them in each of sugar, flour and margarine.)

Whisk the margarine and sugar in a mixer, or by hand, until creamy and smooth. Add the beaten eggs a dessertspoonful at a time (very important). Fold in the sifted flour, then add the vanilla essence. Divide the mixture equally between the tins and bake for 20-25 minutes.

Delicious sandwiched with fresh cream, or whipped cream cheese, with no-sugar jam.

VARIATIONS
Carob Sponge Cake *(illustrated on page 39)*
Just take out 1 tablespoon (15ml) of flour from the Victoria Sandwich recipe and add 1 tablespoon (15ml) of carob powder or carob flour. Sift the carob with the flour to get rid of any lumps.

Chocolate Layer Cake
Just add 2 oz (50g) melted chocolate to the Victoria Sandwich mixture after half the flour has been added.

Whole and Hearty Christmas Cake *(illustrated above)*

You will need a 9in (23cm) cake tin, greased and lined.

Set the oven to 300°F, 150°C, Gas Mark 2.

8oz (225g) polyunsaturated margarine
8oz (225g) Barbados sugar
4 large eggs, separated
12oz (350g) wholemeal flour, plain
1 teaspoon (5ml) grated nutmeg
¼ teaspoon clove powder
juice and rind of 1 large orange
4fl oz (120ml) brandy
8oz (225g) each sultanas, raisins and currants

4oz (110g) dried apricots, chopped
3oz (75g) each crystallised cherries and pineapple
2oz (50g) dried apple, chopped (or apple flakes)
4oz (110g) pecan nuts, chopped
2oz (50g) pecan nuts and 1oz (25g) glacé cherries to decorate

Cream the margarine and sugar for 3 minutes only. Add the beaten egg yolks, then the beaten whites. Add the flour, folding it gently into the mixture. Add the spices, orange rind and juice and 2fl oz (60ml) of the brandy, then add the fruit, first chopping the apricots, apples, cherries and pineapple. Add the nuts, fill the prepared cake tin and decorate with cherries and pecan nuts. Bake for approximately 3 hours. Cool on a wire rack. When cold, pierce in several places with a fine skewer and pour over the remaining brandy.

Special Mincemeat

No sugar or fat needed.

Makes five 1lb (450g) jars.

9oz (250g) dates, steamed and
  chopped
9oz (250g) currants
9oz (250g) raisins
9oz (250g) sultanas
2oz (50g) glacé cherries
2oz (50g) crystallised pineapple
4½oz (125g) candied peel
4½oz (125g) almonds, chopped
4 tablespoons (60ml) brandy, or
  more if liked

4½oz (125g) polyunsaturated
  margarine
1lb (450g) cooking apples (leave
  skins on), grated
grated rind and juice of 1 lemon
grated rind and juice of 1 orange
4½oz (125g) Barbados sugar
  (optional)
½ teaspoon sea salt
1 teaspoon (5ml) nutmeg, grated

Just mix all the ingredients together in a large bowl, stir well and jar in the usual way after two hours.

I find the best pastry to use for mince pies is the basic sweet recipe (see page 18), using an egg yolk to mix.

Plum Pudding

This very simple and tasty mixture will make four 1lb (450g) puddings.

3 level teaspoons (15ml) mixed
  spice
1 level teaspoon (5ml) ground
  ginger
1 level teaspoon (5ml) ground
  cinnamon
6oz (175g) wholemeal flour, plain
6oz (175g) wholemeal
  breadcrumbs
¼ teaspoon sea salt
8oz (225g) polyunsaturated
  margarine
6oz (175g) large raisins, de-seeded

6oz (175g) sultanas
4oz (110g) currants
2oz (50g) mixed peel
2oz (50g) almonds, chopped
8oz (225g) Barbados sugar
4 large eggs, beaten
1 large carrot, grated
1 large cooking apple, with skin
  on, grated
juice and grated rind of 1 lemon
juice and grated rind of 1 small
  orange
½ teaspoon vanilla essence

Mix the spices with the flour, breadcrumbs and salt. Rub in the margarine and add the dried fruit, nuts and sugar. Stir in the beaten eggs. Add the grated apple and carrot. Finally mix in the juice and rind of the lemon and orange and the vanilla essence. Pack into four greased pudding basins and steam for 3 hours. Cover well and store until needed. Steam for 2 to 3 hours before serving.

Note on Steaming The basins should be well greased and only three-quarters full of mixture. Cut out a circle of greaseproof paper or foil larger than the top of the basin and press this under the rim. Place a square of cotton sheeting over the top. Tie some string under the rim, collect the two opposite corners of the cotton square up over the top and tie together, then tie the other two opposite corners of the square to make a handle. Make sure that you have clean paper or foil and a dry, clean cloth on your puddings when storing them.

Swiss Cheesecake *(illustrated on page 39)*

To retain the colour of the cream cheese I use fruit sugar in the filling. Well worth getting for this recipe. A loose-bottomed 9in (23cm) cake tin is essential. Grease the tin well.

Set the oven to 325°F, 160°C, Gas Mark 3.

Base
4oz (110g) polyunsaturated margarine
2½oz (65g) soft dark brown sugar
6oz (175g) wholemeal flour, plain
1 tablespoon (15ml) sesame seeds
pinch of sea salt

Filling
12oz (350g) cream cheese
2oz (50g) fruit sugar
4 eggs, separated
few drops of vanilla essence
grated rind of 1 lemon

juice of ½ lemon
4oz (110g) dried apricots, soaked and puréed (optional, but well worth adding)

Topping
1 small carton sour cream, whipped or 1 small carton double cream, whipped with 1 tablespoon (15ml) thick yoghurt
1oz (25g) flaked almonds, toasted, to decorate

For the base, cream the margarine and sugar for 3 minutes and fold in the flour, sesame seeds and salt. Press the mixture together and then press it into the bottom of the greased tin. Prick the base. Bake for 25 minutes. Leave to cool.

For the filling, cream the cheese and sugar for 3 minutes and gradually add the beaten egg yolks and vanilla. Add the lemon rind and juice. Beat the egg whites until stiff and fold into the mixture. Spread the apricot purée on to the base, pour the cream cheese mixture on top and bake for 1 hour or until the cake is set — check after 45 minutes. If the centre begins to get dark brown when cooking, just cover it with foil and let it cook for the hour, otherwise it tends to be soft. When quite cool spread with the topping and refrigerate for 2 hours before serving. Quite a bother, but worth the effort for special occasions. The lemon juice gives the cheesecake a sharp and delicious flavour.

To make a lighter cheesecake — just as delicious — use 8oz (225g) cream cheese and 8oz (225g) cottage cheese. Sieve the cottage cheese and proceed as above.

Biscuits

Biscuits should be quick to make and a nutritious as well as delicious treat. So here goes with a few nice 'n' easy recipes that are simple to vary and quick to prepare. Remember that the biscuits will still be soft when cooked. They crisp as they cool.

You will notice a similarity between some of the recipes in this short section, but the flavours are quite different. You can vary biscuits very easily. For example, add orange and lemon peel wherever you wish, use muesli base instead of porridge oats for a rougher texture or change nuts for seeds if you feel like it. Bran can be added to biscuits. All you do is take one tablespoon (15ml) of wholemeal flour out, weigh it and put the same amount in weight of bran back into the recipe.

If the biscuits remain a little soft in the middle when cold, just pop them back in the oven for 5 minutes. They will soften but will definitely crisp up when cooled a second time. This shouldn't be necessary but occasionally it does happen.

Malted Sesame Crunchies *(illustrated on page 39)*

You will need three large baking trays, greased and floured.

Makes 24 biscuits.

Set the oven to 300°F, 150°C, Gas Mark 2.

1 heaped teaspoon (10ml) bicarbonate of soda
2 teaspoons (10ml) hot water
4oz (110g) polyunsaturated margarine
1 good tablespoon (20ml) malt

3oz (75g) demerara sugar
3oz (75g) sesame seeds
4oz (110g) wholemeal flour, plain
3oz (75g) porridge oats
pinch of sea salt

Dissolve the bicarbonate of soda in the hot water. Melt the margarine and malt (do not boil). Mix all the dry ingredients together, then mix all the ingredients together. Roll into small balls and place eight on each tray, leaving room for them to spread. They will look small but they spread out considerably while cooking. Bake for 20 minutes. Leave to cool on the baking trays until crisp.

VARIATIONS
Malted Almond Crunchies
Omit the sesame seeds and add 3oz (75g) roughly ground almonds (do not blanch).

Malted Coconut Crunchies
Omit the sesame seeds and add 3oz (75g) desiccated coconut.

The next three recipes are made with sunflower or corn oil instead of margarine. Having run out of margarine one day I used the oil as an experiment, with great success.

(clockwise from top left) Malted
Sesame Crunchies *(lighter colour)*
(see page 37), Pumpkin Seed,
Almond and Honey Snaps
(darker colour) (see page 40),
Carob Sponge Cake (see page
33), Malted Flapjacks (see page
41), Swiss Cheesecake (see page
36), Apricot and Cinnamon
Cake (see page 32).

Carob and Hazel-Nut Munchies

You will need three large baking trays, greased and floured.

Makes 24 biscuits.

Set the oven to 300°F, 150°C, Gas Mark 2.

1 heaped teaspoon (10ml) bicarbonate of soda
2 teaspoons (10ml) hot water
2 tablespoons (30ml) honey
4fl oz (120ml) sunflower oil
grated rind of 1 large orange
3oz (75g) porridge oats

4oz (110g) wholemeal flour, plain
3oz (75g) hazel-nuts, roughly ground
2oz (50g) Barbados sugar, sieved
1 level tablespoon (15ml) carob flour or powder, sieved
pinch of sea salt

Dissolve the bicarbonate of soda in the hot water. Heat the honey and oil (do not boil) and add the orange peel. Mix the dry ingredients, then mix all the ingredients together. Roll into small balls, placing eight on each tray, well spread out. They will spread considerably while cooking. Bake for 20-25 minutes. Leave to cool on the baking trays until crisp.

VARIATIONS
Pumpkin Seed, Almond and Honey Snaps *(illustrated on page 39)*

1 teaspoon (5ml) bicarbonate of soda
2 teaspoons (10ml) hot water
2 tablespoons (30ml) honey
4fl oz (120ml) sunflower oil
3oz (75g) medium oatmeal
4oz (110g) wholemeal flour, plain

1½oz (40g) pumpkin seeds, chopped
1½oz (40g) almonds, roughly chopped
2oz (50g) demerara sugar
pinch of sea salt
2 teaspoons ground ginger

Proceed as in the previous recipe.

Cashew and Cinnamon Chews
Omit the pumpkin seeds, almonds and ginger from the previous recipe and add 3oz (75g) chopped cashews plus 2 teaspoons (10ml) ground cinnamon.

Coconut and Molasses Chompers

These must be the only cookies which don't crumble in your tea. So watch out for your teeth! They are hard cookies to crack. They were very popular in our shop. You will need three large baking trays, greased and floured.

Makes 25 biscuits.

Set the oven to 325°F, 160°C, Gas Mark 3.

4oz (110g) polyunsaturated margarine
2 tablespoons (30ml) molasses
grated rinds of 2 large oranges
8oz (225g) wholemeal flour, plain

6oz (175g) demerara sugar
5oz (150g) desiccated coconut
8oz (225g) porridge oats
pinch of sea salt

Melt the margarine and molasses, stir in the orange rind and add to the dry ingredients. Take up heaped dessertspoonfuls and put them on the prepared trays. Press each gently with a potato masher, leaving room for them to spread while cooking. Bake for 25 minutes.

Malted Flapjacks *(illustrated on page 39)*

Grease and flour one swiss roll tin. Makes 16 good-size flapjacks.

Set the oven to 325°F, 160°C, Gas Mark 3.

4½oz (125g) polyunsaturated margarine
1 good tablespoon (20ml) malt
6oz (175g) demerara sugar
grated rind of ½ lemon

grated rind of ½ orange
12oz (350g) porridge oats
2oz (50g) dried apricots, finely chopped
pinch of sea salt

Melt the margarine, malt and sugar slowly. Do not overheat. Add the orange and lemon rinds and stir, then mix all the ingredients together. Press gently into the swiss roll tin and bake for 35-40 minutes. Cut into squares when still warm.

Wholemeal Shortbread *(illustrated on page 31)*

You will need one large swiss roll tin, greased.

Set the oven to 325°F, 160°C, Gas Mark 3.

8oz (225g) slightly salted butter or polyunsaturated margarine
4oz (110g) soft dark or Barbados sugar, sieved

2 drops vanilla essence
12oz (350g) wholemeal flour, plain
good pinch sea salt

Soften the butter or margarine with a wooden spoon and add the sugar and vanilla essence. Cream for 5 minutes until smooth. Sieve the flour and salt and gradually fold into the creamed mixture. Press together with the hands and flatten it into the tin about ½in (1cm) thick. Prick with a fork and pattern the edges. Mark into slices before cooking. Bake for 40 minutes. Cut through the marked slices and sprinkle with a little dark sugar while still warm.

VARIATION
Carob Shortbread *(illustrated on page 31)*
Take out 1 tablespoons (15ml) wholemeal flour from the previous recipe and add 1 tablespoons (15ml) carob flour or powder. Gives a nice chocolatey taste.

Melting Moments

Very simple, cheap and easy — makes loads.

Set the oven to 350°F, 180°C, Gas Mark 4.

4oz (110g) fruit sugar
8oz (225g) polyunsaturated margarine
1 egg, beaten

few drops vanilla essence
10oz (275g) wholemeal flour, self-raising
2oz (50g) porridge oats

Cream the sugar and margarine for a few minutes then add the egg and vanilla essence. Beat well. Fold in the flour and mix well. Scoop out flat dessertspoonfuls and roll into balls. Dip into the oats and place on a greased baking tray, leaving room to spread a little. Bake for 15-20 minutes.

Whole Grains

POT BARLEY

MILLET

BUCKWHEAT

SURINAM LONG GRAIN
BROWN RICE

ORGANIC
BROWN RICE

CORN OR MAIZE MEAL

LONG GRAIN
BROWN RICE

BULGUR

SHORT GRAIN
BROWN RICE

The Use of Whole Grains

LESSON 4

SHOPPING LIST

Surinam brown rice
Short grain brown rice
Long grain brown rice
Whole grain millet
Bulgur
Buckwheat
Corn or maize meal
Brazil nuts
Sunflower seeds
Soya beans
Pine kernels
Safflower oil

Herbs
Methi (fenugreek leaves)
Sage
Basil
Mint
Bay leaves
Marjoram
Coriander
Curry powder — you can mix your own (see page 100)
Cayenne pepper

I have listed the grains in the order I think best for you to try if you are new to wholefood cookery.

BROWN RICE. Rice grain is similar in structure to wheat grain. It has seven layers which contain all the minerals, protein, fats and vitamins essential for our health. The centre contains carbohydrates and starches. It is easy to digest and has a low gluten and fibre content. In the process of making white rice, the grains have the husk, germ and outer layers removed and finally get polished with glucose or talc so much of the protein, B vitamins and minerals are removed. Brown rice has only the indigestible husks removed.

SURINAM LONG GRAIN BROWN RICE. This rice is very good to start off with as it is quicker to cook than most other varieties and light in texture. It is similar to Basmati rice, which is invariably polished.
Basic cooking method for Surinam rice
Measure out cups of the rice before washing it in a sieve. To 1 cup of Surinam rice add 1½ cups of cold water (it needs less than most other brown rice). Add a little sea salt *or* a stock cube. Bring to the boil then turn down to a gentle simmer, with the lid on, for 25 minutes. Do not stir or the rice will become sticky. When cooked, the rice will have absorbed all the water and be light and fluffy with all the grains separate.

SHORT GRAIN BROWN RICE. Usually the cheapest brown rice and good for both savoury and sweet rice dishes. Marvellous for rice balls.
Basic cooking method for short grain rice
Measure out cups of the rice before washing in a sieve. To 1 cup of short

grain rice add 2 cups of water, bring to the boil, turn down the heat and simmer, with the lid tightly on, for 35-40 minutes maximum.

LONG GRAIN BROWN RICE. This rice is chewy and has a nutty flavour. I use it for any savoury rice dish. Cook as short grain rice.

ORGANICALLY GROWN BROWN RICE. This is superior to non-organic varieties. It is more expensive but worth buying. There are no sprays used and a more gentle process is employed when the outer, indigestible husk is removed. This leaves the sensitive layers undamaged and it is therefore usually more nutritious. Cook as short grain rice.

MILLET — WHOLE GRAIN. Not just for the birds. You deserve it too. This tasty grain is widely used in Africa, India and Asia. Those healthy Hunzas count it as an essential ingredient in their diet. The members of this tribe living in the foothills of the Himalayas are famed for their fitness and longevity. The grain is balanced in essential amino acids, rich in iron, and its protein utilisation value is increased greatly by the addition of vegetables. It is gluten free and makes cake-like bread for those on a gluten-free diet.

Basic cooking method for millet
Heat a very little oil in a thick saucepan and toast the millet in this for a few minutes until it smells nutty and is lightly browned. To 1 cup of millet add 2½ cups of boiling water and a little sea salt. Stir and let it simmer gently for 20 minutes with the lid on all the time. The grains will then be separate and all the water evaporated.

BULGUR. This is a wheat product, highly nutritious and simple to prepare. It is usually sold parboiled, which cuts down the cooking time enormously. The structure of the seed is such that the wheatgerm and bran are retained even when steel milled, because the grain always remains whole. I sometimes use this instead of rice when in a hurry.

Basic preparation for bulgur (no cooking required)
To 1 cup of bulgur add enough boiling water to cover it by ½in (1cm). Add a little shoyu (naturally fermented soy sauce) or a little sea salt to taste. Cover and leave for 15-20 minutes. Your bulgur is now ready to eat.

BUCKWHEAT. This plant is not botanically a grain but is mostly used as one. It contains 11% protein and is rich in iron and the B vitamins. It contains rutic acid which is known to have a powerful effect on the circulatory system and is often prescribed by homeopathic doctors in cases of heart disease, varicose veins, etc. It has a very distinctive, strong flavour so only try this grain when you have got used to brown rice and other whole grains. I love it and use it at least twice a week. I usually get the ready toasted buckwheat as it is quicker to prepare.

Basic cooking method for buckwheat
Heat a little oil in a thick saucepan. Add 1 cup of ready toasted buckwheat and stir for 3 minutes. Add 3 cups of boiling water and a little sea salt. Lid it tightly and simmer for 20 minutes.

CORN MEAL (POLENTA) or MAIZE MEAL. It is important to get stoneground whole corn meal because other products usually have the important germ removed. This grain is rich in vitamin A, phosphorus and potassium. My favourite dish using this grain is Italian Polenta (see page 52). Basic cooking intructions are given in the recipe.

BARLEY (POT BARLEY). Pot barley is the whole grain, which contains the bran and germ. It has more flavour than pearl barley which is polished and lacks most of the bran and germ. Barley is easily digested and therefore good for babies and those who have digestive disorders — great added to stews or used instead of rice.
Basic cooking method for barley
Wash it well and soak overnight for the best results. To 1 cup of barley add 2½ cups of water and soak for at least 6 hours. Add a little sea salt, bring to the boil and simmer for 30 minutes with the lid on.

Brown Rice

You will find more dishes using brown rice in the lessons on Pulses and Indian Cuisine.

Rice and Vegetable Bake (with toasted cashews)

You will need one large casserole dish without a lid.

Set the oven to 375°F, 190°C, Gas Mark 5.

Serves 5.

12oz (350g) (dry weight) long grain Italian rice, cooked with a vegetable stock cube for 35 minutes only and drained (see page 44)
4oz (110g) cashews or **pine kernels**
4 tablespoons (60ml) sunflower or **olive oil**
1 large onion, peeled and finely chopped
2 cloves garlic, crushed
2 medium carrots, scrubbed and cut into 1in (2cm) sticks
3 sticks celery, finely chopped
1 medium courgette, washed and sliced (optional)
½ medium green pepper, de-seeded and chopped

½ medium red pepper, de-seeded and chopped
4oz (110g) button mushrooms, washed and sliced
2 tablespoons (30ml) parsley, chopped
1 teaspoon (5ml) dried basil
1 level teaspoon (5ml) dried tarragon
14oz (396g) can tomatoes, chopped
freshly ground black pepper
1 tablespoon (15ml) shoyu (naturally fermented soy sauce)
5oz (150g) farmhouse Cheddar cheese, grated
sprigs of parsley or **watercress to garnish**

Toast the cashews in a dry, thick pan for 3 minutes, stirring them with a wooden spoon until lightly browned. Fork them into the rice. Sauté the onion, garlic and carrots for 5 minutes in the oil, then add the celery and sauté for another 5 minutes. Add the courgettes, peppers and mushrooms, parsley, basil and tarragon. Sauté for 3 minutes. Add the tomatoes and juice, black pepper and shoyu. Stir gently and heat for 1 more minute, then fork the mixture into the rice. Take care not to make it mushy. Sprinkle the grated cheese and a little more basil on the top and bake for 30 minutes. Garnish with sprigs of parsley or watercress.

Best served with a green salad or lightly cooked spinach.

Opposite *(top)* Bulgur Salad, (Lebanese style) (see page 53), *(right)* Peach Chutney (see page 126), *(bottom)* Curried Rice and Chick Pea Balls (see page 48).

Curried Rice and Chick Pea Balls *(illustrated on page 47)*

These are delicious served hot with a salad and Peach Chutney (see page 126) or cold for a buffet party. You will need a frying pan with enough soya or corn oil for semi-deep frying.

Makes 15.

1lb (450g) short grain Italian rice, cooked (see page 44)
1 medium onion, peeled and finely chopped
1 rounded tablespoon (20ml) hot curry powder
1 dessertspoon (10ml) methi or sage
4oz (110g) ground Brazil nuts

5oz (150g) chick peas, cooked (see page 60 on cooking beans)
1 tablespoon (15ml) lemon juice
1 tablespoon (15ml) shoyu (naturally fermented soy sauce)
1 egg yolk
oil for semi-deep frying

Cook the rice well. There should be no water left, but drain it in a large sieve just in case. Sauté the onion until soft, add the curry powder, methi or sage, stir and sauté for 1 more minute. Mix all the other ingredients except the egg yolk together while the rice is still hot. Lastly mix in the egg yolk. This helps to stop the rice balls falling apart in the pan. Stick the mixture well together with your hands and form into golf ball size pieces, very slightly flatten them and semi-deep fry a few at a time in very hot oil. The rice balls should be half submerged. When one side is golden brown pop them over with a fork, and cook the other side. Drain on kitchen paper. Keep warm in the oven.

VARIATION
Rice Balls with Toasted Sunflower Seeds

1lb (450g) short grain Italian rice, cooked (see page 44)
4oz (110g) sunflower seeds, toasted
2oz (50g) wholemeal breadcrumbs
1 large onion, peeled, finely chopped and sautéd

2 tablespoons (30ml) parsley, chopped
2 tablespoons (30ml) shoyu (naturally fermented soy sauce)
2 tablespoons (30ml) lemon juice
1 egg yolk

Mix all the ingredients together and proceed as above.

Rice with Soya Beans and Watercress

If you have the soya beans ready cooked and frozen this tasty rice is beautifully simple to prepare, delicious hot or cold, either as a main dish full of protein or as a buffet salad bowl. See page 77 for cooking soya beans and page 44 for cooking Surinam rice.

Serves 4.

10oz (275g) (dry weight) Surinam rice, cooked
6oz (175g) (dry weight) soya beans, cooked
2 tomatoes, skinned and chopped
1 tablespoon (15ml) tomato purée
1 clove garlic, crushed
1 small onion, finely chopped
4oz (110g) button mushrooms, washed and sliced
1 courgette, washed and thinly sliced
2 tablespoons (30ml) corn oil for frying

1 tablespoon (15ml) fresh parsley, chopped
¼ teaspoon dry mustard powder
1 dessertspoon (10ml) coriander powder
1 tablespoon (15ml) shoyu (naturally fermented soy sauce)
2 bunches watercress, trimmed and chopped (leave the stems on)
chopped parsley to garnish

The rice should be all separate and free from any excess water. If the soya beans are frozen, just put boiling water over them and drain. Liquidise the tomatoes with the tomato purée, garlic and onion. Sauté the mushrooms and courgette in the oil for just 3 minutes, add the tomato mixture, then add the parsley, mustard and coriander. Stir in well. Add the cooked soya beans and heat through for 2 minutes. Add the soy sauce and stir over a low heat for 1 minute. Take off the heat and fork in the chopped watercress. Finally fork in the cooked rice — take care not to mash it together. Heat through and serve hot, garnished with chopped parsley, or leave to get cold for a buffet. We like Peach Chutney with this. See page 126 for the recipe.

VARIATION
Use any cooked beans such as black eye or haricot instead of soya beans. This recipe can also be used for stuffing marrows or other vegetables.

Stuffed Spinach Leaves

This recipe is adapted from a Middle Eastern dish. You can substitute vine or cabbage leaves but I prefer spinach. I have used pine kernels but you can substitute chopped, blanched almonds if the pine nuts are too difficult to obtain. They are worth trying for. Make sure you get shelled nuts, otherwise you will spend hours preparing them. You will need a large baking dish, greased, to take 20 filled spinach leaves.

Set the oven to 375°F, 190°C, Gas Mark 5.

Serves 4.

20 spinach leaves — approx 8oz (225g) fresh spinach, cooked in boiling, salt water for 2 minutes. Pick each leaf out as required.

Filling
8oz (225g) Surinam rice, cooked (see page 44)
1 large onion, peeled and finely chopped
2 cloves garlic, minced
3 tablespoons (45ml) sunflower or olive oil
4oz (110g) button mushrooms, washed and finely chopped
1 tablespoon (15ml) fresh parsley, finely chopped
1 large sprig fresh mint, chopped or 1 teaspoon (5ml) dried mint
1 level tablespoon (15ml) coriander powder
4 medium tomatoes, skinned and chopped
2oz (50g) shelled pine kernels or blanched almonds, chopped
juice of ½ lemon

Sauce
1½ pints (850ml) basic white sauce (see pages 121-2)
6oz (175g) cottage cheese, sieved or curd cheese
cayenne pepper

All the water should be absorbed by the rice. If not, leave the rice in a sieve to drain. Sauté the onion and garlic in the oil for 7 minutes. Add the mushrooms and sauté for 3 minutes. Add the parsley, mint and coriander. Continue to cook for 1 minute. Add the tomatoes and pine kernels or almonds. Stir gently and then pour the mixture into the cooked rice. Do not mash together. Fork in the lemon juice. Put one of the spinach leaves on a plate and spoon 1 tablespoon of the rice mixture on to it. Make a parcel by folding the long sides over the mixture and rolling it lengthwise. It will stick well together. Make 20 parcels and place in the baking dish. Add the curd or sieved cottage cheese to the hot white sauce. Do not cook, just stir it in, and pour the sauce over the spinach packets. Sprinkle a little cayenne pepper over the top and bake for 30 minutes.

Serve with salad, or as a delicious starter without the cheese sauce. When serving as a starter just make into packets, keep warm in a covered dish and sprinkle with lemon juice when serving.

Opposite Toasted Buckwheat Savoury with Almonds (see page 54), Millet and Cheese Croquettes.

Millet

Millet and Cheese Croquettes

These are very tasty and nutritious served with chutney and salad. You will need enough oil to semi-deep fry. A large, thick frying pan is best — do not use a chip pan. Makes 10.

8oz (225g) whole grain millet, cooked (see page 45)
4oz (110g) Cheddar cheese, grated
1 dessertspoon (10ml) dried sage
1 medium onion, peeled, chopped and sautéd

1 level teaspoon (5ml) cayenne pepper
1 egg yolk

When the millet is cooked and still hot add the cheese, sage, sautéd onion and cayenne pepper. Stir in well, add the egg yolk and press the mixture firmly together like a dough. Form into ten balls and press them into croquette shapes by flattening to 1in (2·5cm) thick. Have enough oil in the pan to come to just over half way up the croquettes. The oil must be very hot, as for chips, before putting the croquettes in. When a deep golden brown turn over and cook the other side. If the croquettes tend to break up just brush them with a little beaten egg before frying.

Children seem to like these best without the cayenne, made into little flat patties and fried in a little oil as you would do sauté potatoes.

Millet and Mushroom Bake

You will need a large, greased casserole dish with a tight lid.

Set the oven to 350°F, 180°C, Gas Mark 4.

Serves 4.

3 tablespoons (45ml) oil for frying
8oz (225g) whole grain millet
2 medium carrots, scrubbed and cut in 1in (2·5cm) thick sticks
1 large onion or 2 medium size, peeled and chopped
1 clove garlic, crushed
6oz (175g) button mushrooms, washed and sliced
1 tablespoon (15ml) fresh parsley, chopped

1 teaspoon (5ml) lemon thyme or thyme
1½ pints (850ml) good hot stock (add 1½ vegetable stock cubes to boiling water if you have no stock)
1 small aubergine, thinly sliced in rings (optional)
2 medium tomatoes, thinly sliced in rings
4oz (110g) Cheddar cheese, grated

Put 1 tablespoon (15ml) of the oil in a large, thick saucepan and heat it well. Add the millet, and toast it for 5 minutes until lightly browned. Transfer to the greased casserole dish. Sauté the carrot, onion and garlic in the remaining oil for 3 minutes. Add the mushrooms and sauté for 2 minutes only. Stir in the parsley and lemon thyme or thyme. Fork this vegetable mixture into the toasted millet. Pour on the stock and stir gently. Pop the slices of aubergine and tomato on top of the liquid. They will float a bit but will settle on top later. Sprinkle the cheese on top of this, cover with the tight lid and bake for 1 hour.

Corn or Maize Meal

Italian Polenta *(illustrated on page 55)*

You will need a large square ovenproof dish, greased.

Set the oven to 375°F, 190°C, Gas Mark 5.

Serves 6.

6oz (175g) corn meal
1 teaspoon (5ml) sea salt
½ pint (275ml) cold water
1 pint (550ml) boiling water
oil for frying
1 large onion, peeled and finely chopped
2 cloves garlic, crushed
1 medium green pepper, de-seeded and chopped
1 small aubergine, chopped (optional)

1 medium courgette, sliced (optional)
4oz (110g) button mushrooms, washed and sliced
1 teaspoon (5ml) dried mint
1 teaspoon (5ml) celery seeds
1 teaspoon (5ml) herb salt
freshly ground black pepper
14oz (396g) can tomatoes
2 tablespoons (30ml) tomato purée
2oz (50g) sunflower seeds
4oz (110g) Cheddar cheese, grated

Mix the corn meal, sea salt and cold water together. Add this to the boiling water, stirring well. Bring to the boil, stirring continuously and simmer for 5 minutes. Stir once or twice while simmering. Place in the ovenproof dish. Sauté the onion and garlic for 7 minutes. Add the green pepper, aubergine, courgette and mushrooms. Sauté for 5 minutes then add the mint, celery seeds, herb salt and pepper. Stir in well and add the tomatoes, tomato purée and sunflower seeds. Simmer for 20 minutes with the lid on, then spread over the corn meal. Sprinkle with cheese and bake for 30 minutes.

Bulgur

Bulgur Salad (Lebanese style) *(illustrated on page 47)*

This is one of my favourite ways of eating bulgur as a cold salad dish. Lovely for a light lunch or main meal served with curd or cottage cheese.

Serves 6-8.

8oz (225g) bulgur, plus 1 tablespoon (15ml) shoyu (naturally fermented soy sauce)
2 tablespoons (30ml) cold pressed safflower oil or olive oil
2 tablespoons (30ml) fresh lemon juice
½ teaspoon freshly ground black pepper
sea salt
¼ teaspoon mustard powder

2 cloves garlic, crushed
4oz (110g) spring onions, chopped or Spanish onion, finely chopped
4 tablespoons (60ml) parsley, finely chopped
1 dessertspoon (10ml) dried mint or, even better, a few sprigs fresh mint, finely chopped
4 medium tomatoes, chopped
watercress and lettuce leaves to serve

Soak the bulgur in enough boiling water to cover it by 1in (2·5cm) and add the soy sauce. Lid the dish while it is soaking. Your bulgur is then cooked. Bulgur must be cold before mixing with fresh vegetables. Mix the oil, lemon juice, pepper, salt, mustard and garlic well together. Mix all the other ingredients together in a large bowl and then pour over the oil dressing. Toss the mixture gently together.

Lay the salad in a large platter and surround it with watercress and lettuce leaves. Add a little parsley to garnish. Serve with curd or cottage cheese. I add a sprinkle of cayenne pepper on the cheese to give it a slightly hot, peppery taste.

If in a hurry I sometimes use bulgur instead of rice and find that most recipes where rice is required are equally successful using this grain as an alternative.

Opposite Italian Polenta (see page 52).

Buckwheat

Toasted Buckwheat Savoury with Almonds

(illustrated on page 50)

You will need just one good, thick saucepan and one frying pan. Serves 4.

1 cup toasted buckwheat (approx 5oz (150g))	4 large tomatoes, skinned and chopped
2 bay leaves	1 tablespoon (15ml) fresh parsley, chopped
a little sea salt	
1 large onion, peeled and chopped	1 teaspoon (5ml) marjoram
2 cloves garlic, crushed	3 dessertspoons (30ml) shoyu (naturally fermented soy sauce)
oil for frying	
4oz (110g) button mushrooms, washed and sliced	3oz (75g) sliced almonds, toasted
1 small red or green pepper, de-seeded and chopped	sprigs of watercress to garnish

Cook the buckwheat (see page 45) with the bay leaves and a little sea salt. Sauté the onion and garlic until soft, add the mushrooms and peppers and sauté for just 3 minutes. Add the tomatoes and sauté for 1 minute. Add the parsley and marjoram and finally the soy sauce. Stir a couple of times and then either fork into the hot buckwheat or pour into the centre of a ring of buckwheat ready to fork in just before serving. Toast the almonds in a dry pan for 3-5 minutes, stirring all the time, until lightly browned. Put the buckwheat mixture in a hot serving dish and sprinkle the toasted almonds on top. Garnish with sprigs of watercress.

Delicious with Orange, Tomato and Onion Salad (see page 113).

Barley

I use barley as an alternative grain in some rice dishes. For example, barley is really delicious used in the Rice and Vegetable Bake recipe (see page 46). Just omit the rice and use barley instead.

The recipes for this lesson using these grains will, I hope, encourage you to experiment for yourself. They have all been tried out and much appreciated and are simple to prepare once you have mastered the art of cooking different grains.

LESSON 5

Pulses (Beans, Peas and Lentils)

SHOPPING LIST

Butter beans
Tahini (sesame seed paste)
Red kidney beans
Mung beans
Soya (TVP) mince, beef flavour
Pinto beans

Red or any other lentils

Herbs and Spices
Rosemary
Cumin

Beans, peas and lentils provide a good, cheap source of protein. The protein content ranges from 17 per cent to 25 per cent with the exception of the soya bean which has approximately 38 per cent protein. I have devoted a complete lesson to the soya bean (see page 76) because of its outstanding nutritional qualities and variable uses. Pulses are also a very good source of vitamins and minerals, namely iron, calcium and vitamin B_1, thiamine and niacin. Vitamin C is present only when the pulses are sprouted.

The protein in these wonderful dried vegetables used to be regarded as 'second class'. Only the soya bean contains all the amino acids which the body requires to build protein, but through much research it has been found that pulses used in combination with certain other foods which contain the missing amino acids will produce a complete protein with all the amino acids in balance. The foods which contain these missing proteins are whole grains, nuts, seeds and all dairy produce. Using any of these with pulses will provide you with the necessary complete protein. Rest assured that if you make grains approximately 50 per cent of your main meal, nuts, seeds, beans or dairy produce 25 per cent and with the remaining 25 per cent consisting of fresh vegetables, raw or steamed, you will be eating enough well balanced protein. This balancing is often instinctive and particularly apparent in traditional Eastern and Middle Eastern dishes. Unfortunately, with the increasing tendency to process wholefoods in the West, and to some extent in the East, we are in danger of clouding our instincts and our food is straying a long way from its natural state.

Eating more pulses and consequently a little less meat will help not only your purse and your health but our planet to survive. Remember that a harvest of soya beans from one acre of land will provide enough protein for one person for six years. The same harvest fed to animals will provide adequate protein for one human being for only eighty days.

Soaking and Cooking Pulses

All raw peas and beans (both fresh and dried) contain substances such as glycosides, saponins and alkaloids which are harmful to digestion. When they are fresh just five minutes cooking will be sufficient to render the substances harmless and when using the dried variety proper soaking, rinsing and cooking for the right length of time will stop any action of the poisonous substances.

As a general rule I soak all beans overnight — even the smaller varieties such as mung and aduki. I then drain off the water, rinse them well and add fresh water before cooking. This process inhibits the action of any adverse substances that could play havoc with your intestines. The cooking time will vary according to the size and variety of bean you are using. Lentils, of course, do not need soaking but I pick them well over for small stones, as I do all beans, and pour boiling water over them, leave for 10 minutes, drain and add fresh water before cooking. Do not add salt to beans until 10 minutes before the end of the cooking time to prevent toughening of the outer skins. Never add bicarbonate of soda — it might soften the beans but it can destroy valuable nutrients, as well as ruining their natural, individual and delicate flavour.

If beans are not stored properly in an airtight container away from direct sunlight, or are old stock, they will not only take ages to cook but will have absorbed moisture and smells from the atmosphere, which will make them unpleasant to taste. So be sure to get your pulses from a shop which has a quick turnover.

One last important point. Add pulses to your diet slowly. One new variety each week will help your body to adjust to a new way of eating.

ADUKI BEANS. 'The King of Beans' is the grand title given to these little red beans by the Japanese. They originated from Japan and have been widely used there and in China for centuries, both for culinary and medicinal purposes. The juice from the cooked bean is said to be a cure for kidney complaints and an aid to regulating the menstrual cycle. I found this variety comparatively easy to digest when I first began to incorporate pulses regularly into my daily diet, and its meaty taste went down well with the family.
Basic cooking method for aduki beans
Soak for four hours or overnight. Rinse off the soaking water and add fresh water to cover before cooking. Boil for 10 minutes with the lid on, then simmer gently for a further 30 minutes. Add salt 10 minutes before the end of the cooking time. If these beans are very fresh they might take less time to cook as they are small and do not have a tough skin, so check after 30 minutes.

BLACK EYED BEANS (OR PEAS). These beans are a staple food in Africa. They have a distinctive, nutty flavour and go well in stuffed cabbage, spinach or vine leaves as an alternative to the very expensive pine kernels, which are often an ingredient in these recipes. They are also delicious in spicy rice dishes.
Basic cooking methods for black eyed beans (or peas)
Soak overnight, rinse and add fresh water to cook the beans. Bring to the boil and keep boiling with the lid on for 10 minutes, then simmer for a further 35 minutes or until soft. Add sea salt 10 minutes before the end of the cooking time.

BLACK KIDNEY BEANS

RED SPLIT LENTILS   FLAGEOLET BEANS

BLACK EYED BEANS   ADUKI BEANS

CONTINENTAL
(GREEN) LENTILS

SPLIT YELLOW AND
GREEN PEAS

CHICK PEAS

RED KIDNEY BEANS

HARICOT BEANS

BROWN LENTILS

BUTTER BEANS

MUNG BEANS

PINTO BEANS

BUTTER BEANS (OR LIMA BEANS — a smaller version). As the name suggests, these beans originated from Lima in Peru. I find they are very popular, probably because of their mild, buttery, potato flavour. (See the recipes on page 64 for Butter Bean Casseroles. Most kids like them.)
Basic cooking method for butter, or lima, beans
It is very important to soak these particular beans overnight and change the soaking water at least once. Rinse well after soaking and add fresh water to cook. Boil vigorously for 10 minutes then simmer for a further 40 minutes or until the beans are soft. They can go too mushy, so test after 35 minutes for softness.

The reason for extra care in cooking some beans such as these, red kidney beans and soya beans is that some varieties have more adverse substances in them in their raw state than others. Do not be put off using them because of this. You will miss out, especially where the soya bean is concerned, on such a wonderful protein, vitamin and mineral boost to your diet. Just take care in the preparation and cooking and there will be no ill effects.

CHICK PEAS (OR GURBANZO PEAS). These fabulous peas, thought to have originated in western Asia, are one of my favourites. They are so versatile and tasty. Try the recipe for Falafal with a delicious sauce on page 65 and Hummous (page 128).
Chick pea flour (gram flour) is fantastic used on its own or with soya and brown rice flour for battered vegetables (see page 105) or fish.
Basic cooking method for chick peas
Soak overnight in plenty of water, say 3 pints to 1·1lb (500g) of peas as they swell up more than most during soaking. Rinse well and add fresh water to cook. Boil for 10 minutes then simmer for 50 minutes. Add sea salt 10 minutes before the end of the cooking time. Taste one when they are cooked but don't let the family have any or you might find you have none left for your recipe!

FLAGEOLET BEANS. These are young kidney beans. They are delicate in flavour and absolutely delicious either eaten as a salad with French dressing or in cooked dishes.
Basic cooking method for flageolet beans
As these are not so widely used you have to be careful that these beans have not been on the shelf for too long a time. Soak overnight, rinse and add fresh water to cook. Boil for 5 minutes. Simmer for 40 minutes, but check after 30 minutes because if they are freshly dried they will cook quite quickly. Add only a very little salt just 10 minutes before the end of the cooking time. Search for these beans or pester your usual supplier. They are a real treat.

HARICOT BEANS (WHITE VARIETY). These small, white, mild-flavoured beans are delicious with my tasty Barbecue Sauce (see page 124). I often use them in a mixed bean salad with red kidney beans but take care to cook them separately as they take longer than the red variety and take on a pinkish colour if cooked together, thus spoiling the look of the finished salad.
Basic cooking method for haricot beans
Soak overnight or longer, drain, rinse and add fresh water to cook. Bring

to the boil, let them boil for 10 minutes then simmer for 55-60 minutes more. Check after 45 minutes for softness. Add sea salt 10 minutes before the cooking is finished.

KIDNEY BEANS (RED OR BLACK VARIETY). These popular beans, often used in hot chilli dishes, have been cultivated in Mexico and South America for well over 7,000 years. Note the cooking instructions well as these beans contain more adverse substances than most pulses, as previously mentioned in the butter bean notes. Do not be put off using kidney beans because of this, as proper preparation and cooking will render the substances harmless. (See page 67 for a simple salad recipe with red kidney and flageolet beans. Also Stuffed Spinach Pancakes with Kidney Beans on page 69.)
Basic cooking method for kidney beans
Soak overnight, changing the water at least once. Rinse well and add fresh water to cook. Boil vigorously for 10 minutes, then simmer for a further 50 minutes. Sometimes these beans cook quite quickly so check after 40 minutes or you might find that they are overdone. You could end with mushy beans which are not good to use in salads. Salt the beans 10 minutes before the end of the cooking time.

MUNG BEANS. Another of my favourite beans — great for sprouting. These are what the Chinese mainly use when sprouting beans for commercial supply, but whatever I do I cannot get mine to sprout as long as theirs. There must be some secret, but maybe it is best that we do not know it! This bean originated in India and gradually spread throughout Asia. The beans are often made into a flour called green gram — not to be confused with chick pea flour which is gram. I love mung beans as the basic ingredient in a vegetarian Shepherds' Pie (see recipe on page 72).
Basic cooking method for mung beans
Soak overnight then rinse and cook in fresh water. Boil for 5 minutes then simmer for 30-35 minutes only. These are another bean I found easy to digest when starting my bean cuisine in earnest.

PINTO BEANS. These lovely-flavoured, speckled beans are great in casseroles and bean salads. They are similar to the butter bean but slightly stronger tasting. I also like them in a bean loaf (see page 72 for the recipe) or bean rissoles. They are from the kidney bean family and have been cultivated by North and South American Indians since prehistoric times.
Basic cooking method for pinto beans
Soak overnight, rinse well and cook in fresh water. Boil for 10 minutes then simmer for another 40 minutes or until soft. Add sea salt 10 minutes before the end of the cooking time.

LENTILS AND SPLIT PEAS. I will just list these pulses with basic cooking instructions as I am sure most readers will be familiar with cooking them.
Basic cooking method for lentils and split peas
Soak in boiling water for about 1 hour, then drain, rinse and cook as the recipe directs.

SPLIT YELLOW OR GREEN PEAS. Delicious in soups and casseroles. You can get a green pea flour in some wholefood stores which is great for thickening soups such as leek. Add about one rounded tablespoon (20ml) per pint (550ml) by mixing to a paste with a little cold water and then mixing thoroughly with a small quantity of the soup before blending into the main volume. It adds a lovely flavour as well as extra nourishment.

RED SPLIT LENTILS. One of the first crops to be cultivated in the East — again lovely in a soup, lightly spiced and with lemon juice (see page 119 for the recipe). They make a really lovely dhal which often accompanies the main meal in Indian cuisine (see page 102). I also like Lentil Bake, which is nice eaten hot with mushroom sauce or cold with salad (see page 74).

BROWN LENTILS. These lentils are the red lentil variety unsplit and with the outer skin still on. They have a natural spicy flavour.

GREEN LENTILS (CONTINENTAL LENTILS). Delicious made into a thick broth or as a change of flavour when making a dhal.

Well, that's a bumper lot of pulses to be getting on with. Just go slowly and incorporate them gradually into your diet.

Opposite *(left)* Hot Flageolet Bean Salad (see page 145), *(right)* Aduki Burgers.

Aduki Beans

Aduki Burgers *(illustrated opposite)*

Makes 8.

4oz (110g) porridge oats	1 clove garlic, crushed
6oz (175g) (dry weight) aduki beans, soaked, cooked and well drained (see page 57 on cooking beans)	2 tablespoons (30ml) tomato purée
	2 tablespoons (30ml) shoyu (naturally fermented soy sauce)
1 medium onion, peeled and very finely chopped	½ teaspoon freshly ground black pepper
2 tablespoons (30ml) parsley, chopped	1 beaten egg to bind
	toasted porridge oats to coat
1 teaspoon (5ml) basil	a little oil for frying

Toast the porridge oats in a moderate oven for 10 minutes only. Mash the cooked beans and mix all the ingredients together with the egg. Squash well together and form into burgers ½in (1cm) thick. Roll each in a few toasted oats. Sauté in a little oil for 4 minutes on each side. Do not add more oats because this will make the burgers too dry when cooked.

Delicious served with a white sauce (see pages 121-2), steamed sprouts, broccoli or cauliflower and jacket potatoes. They are also delicious cold for packed lunches or picnics.

Butter or Lima Beans

Butter Bean Casserole 1

You will need one casserole dish without a lid.

Set the oven to 375°F, 190°C, Gas Mark 5.

Serves 4.

8oz (225g) butter beans, soaked and cooked (see page 60 for cooking instructions)
2 medium onions, peeled and finely chopped
3 sticks celery, finely chopped
2 tablespoons (30ml) sunflower oil
1 tablespoon (30ml) fresh parsley, chopped
1 level teaspoon (5ml) dried rosemary or oregano
1 clove garlic, crushed
5 tomatoes, skinned and chopped
1 tablespoon (30ml) shoyu (naturally fermented soy sauce)
freshly ground black pepper
4 largish potatoes, steamed or baked with jackets on (cook extra potatoes the day before and save them)
4oz (110g) Cheddar cheese, grated

Cook the beans and reserve 7fl oz (200ml) of the cooking liquid. Put the cooked beans in the casserole dish with the cooking liquid. Sauté the onion and celery in the oil for 5 minutes and add the parsley, rosemary or oregano and the garlic. Stir well in, then add the tomatoes, shoyu and pepper. Heat through and fork into the butter beans. Slice the potatoes, leaving the skins on, and place, overlapping each other, over the bean mixture. Sprinkle with the grated cheese. Bake for 30-35 minutes until golden brown.

Butter Bean Casserole 2

Set the oven to 375°F, 190°C, Gas Mark 5.

Serves 4.

8oz (225g) (dry weight) butter beans or Lima beans
1 vegetable stock cube
1 tablespoon (15ml) wholemeal flour, plain, mixed with a little cold water
¼ teaspoon dry mustard powder
1 tablespoon (15ml) parsley, chopped
½ teaspoon celery seeds
¼ teaspoon freshly ground black pepper
4oz (110g) yoghurt cheese (see page 130 for making this)
3 medium leeks, washed and cut into ½in (1cm) lengths
savoury crumble mix for top, made with 8oz (225g) wholemeal flour (see page 19)

Soak and cook the beans (see page 60), making sure that you have approximately 7fl oz (200ml) of liquid left in the beans when cooked. Instead of adding sea salt, stir in the vegetable stock cube mixed with the flour mixture 10 minutes before the end of the cooking time. Fork in the mustard powder and parsley, celery seeds, black pepper and yoghurt cheese and empty the mixture into a casserole dish. Press the chopped leeks into the bean mixture, keeping the leek pieces whole. Cover with the savoury crumble mix. Bake for 40 minutes until browned. If the crumble seems to be getting brown too quickly turn the oven down — 40 minutes cooking time is necessary to cook the leeks.

Chick Peas

Falafal (Ground Chick Pea Balls)

A traditional Middle Eastern delight. Serve on a bed of fresh lettuce with pitta bread and yoghurt. This recipe is a real treat — well worth the bother.

Makes 30-40.

1· 1lb (500g) (dry weight) chick peas, cooked and drained (see page 60)
1 heaped teaspoon (10ml) ground coriander
4 tablespoons (60ml) olive oil
2 tablespoons (30ml) fresh parsley, finely chopped
3 large cloves garlic, crushed
2 tablespoons (30ml) tahini
juice of 2 lemons (approx 4 tablespoons (60ml))

½ teaspoon freshly ground black pepper
sea salt to taste
1 level teaspoon (5ml) cayenne pepper or chilli powder (optional but adds that extra umph!)
1 egg, beaten to bind
wholemeal flour, plain, for coating
vegetable oil for deep frying

Drain the chick peas well. Discard the water and grate the chick peas through either a hand or electric cheese grater. Soft, powdery flakes will form. Do not add any water. Add all the other ingredients, leaving the beaten egg until last. Form into walnut-size balls, making approximately 40. Roll each in wholemeal flour and deep fry for 3 minutes in hot oil. Drain on kitchen paper and keep warm in the oven.

Delicious served with Yoghurt Bowl Cooler (see page 130) or with my special Chilli Tomato Sauce (see page 124). You can add 4oz (110g) wholemeal breadcrumbs to this recipe to make a more complete protein meal.

Spicy Chick Peas with Bulgur

Delicious hot or cold.

Serves 6.

8oz (225g) bulgur, soaked (see page 45)
8oz (225g) chick peas, soaked and cooked (see page 60)

curry sauce (see page 125)

All you do is to place the prepared bulgur on a large serving dish, making a slight well in the middle. Stir the chick peas into the curry sauce and simmer for 5-10 minutes on a low heat. Pour the sauce and peas into the centre of the bulgur. Serve with yoghurt cheese (see page 130) or thick yoghurt.

Chick Pea, Tomato and Tarragon Casserole

*Use fresh tomatoes when in season.
This dish is very simple and easy to
prepare and delicious hot or cold.*

Serves 4.

12oz (350g) soft, ripe tomatoes
(canned tomatoes can be used)
3 tablespoons (45ml) olive oil
1 medium onion, peeled and
chopped
2 cloves garlic, crushed
1 teaspoon (5ml) ground coriander
1 teaspoon (5ml) basil

1 teaspoon (5ml) dried tarragon (if
fresh used, double the amount)
1 tablespoon (15ml) fresh parsley,
chopped
sea salt
freshly ground black pepper
8oz (225g) (dry weight) chick peas,
cooked (see page 60)

Skin the tomatoes by cutting a circle around the edge of the stalk end and
blanch in boiling water for 5 minutes. The skin will then peel off easily.
Chop them well. Heat the oil and sauté the onion and garlic for 10
minutes until soft. Cover the pan with a lid while frying. Add the
peppers, coriander, basil, tarragon and parsley and continue to fry for a
further 2 minutes only. Stir in the chopped tomatoes and add salt and
pepper to taste. Combine the peas with the tomato mixture and place in a
casserole dish, cover tightly and bake at 300°F, 150°C, Gas Mark 2 for
1½ hours. (You can bake it on a slightly higher temperature for 1 hour
only, but I prefer to cook the casserole more slowly so that the chick peas
absorb the flavour of the sauce.)

    This is delicious stirred into bulgur (see page 45) with a sprinkling of
lemon juice and garnished with fresh chopped parsley and mint.

Chick Pea Fritters

*Again, a variation of the Falafal
mixture but a slightly different
method, much quicker to make.*

Makes about 12.

8oz (225g) (dry weight) chick peas,
cooked and drained (see page 60)
1 medium onion, peeled and finely
chopped
oil for frying
4oz (110g) porridge oats
2 tablespoons (30ml) fresh parsley,
chopped
2 tablespoons (30ml) fresh lemon
juice

1 tablespoon (15ml) tahini
1 clove garlic (optional)
freshly ground black pepper and
sea salt to taste
1 egg to bind
bowl of porridge oats or medium
oatmeal to coat

Mash the cooked and drained chick peas with a potato masher. They will
be roughly mashed and bumpy but that is all right for this recipe, it gives
a nice texture and taste to the finished fritters. Sauté the onion for just 5
minutes until soft but not brown. Mix all the ingredients together,
leaving the egg until last. Squash well with the hands. The mixture
should be soft but manageable, not stiff. The fritters firm up when you fry
them. Form the mixture into flattish rounds about ½in (1cm) deep and
3in (8cm) in diameter, dip in porridge oats or medium oatmeal to coat
and fry in very shallow oil for 3 minutes each side. Use a fish slice and pop
them over carefully when one side is golden brown.

    Delicious served with fresh salad or any steamed vegetables. Make
loads of them — you will never have enough.

Haricot Beans (White)

These beans are quite bland in flavour so I invariably use them with other beans such as in the Bean Salad Bowl recipe below, or with a really flavoursome Barbecue Sauce.

Bean Salad Bowl

My choice of beans look colourful and inviting as well as complementing each other in taste.

Cook the beans separately — this is very important. See pages 60-1 for cooking instructions.

4oz (110g) (dry weight) red kidney beans, cooked

4oz (110g) (dry weight) haricot beans, cooked

4oz (110g) (dry weight) flageolet beans, cooked

Do not overcook the beans. Drain them well and fork the mixture together gently, with a wooden fork if possible. While still warm, but not hot, pour on Yoghurt Cheese or Sour Cream Dressing (see page 114) or traditional French dressing.

Haricot Beans with Barbecue Sauce

1· 1lb (500g) (dry weight) haricot beans, cooked and drained (see page 60)

1 pint (550ml) Barbecue Sauce (see page 124)

Just pour the hot sauce over the hot, cooked beans and let the family tuck in. Great on toasted wholemeal bread or with soya burgers and mash.

Haricot Beans, Courgettes and Mushrooms au Gratin

You can use flageolet beans for this recipe if you wish. They take less time to cook than haricot beans but are more expensive.

Set the oven to 325°F, 160°C, Gas Mark 3.

Serves 4.

3 tablespoons (45ml) olive oil or sunflower oil

1 large onion, peeled and chopped

2 cloves garlic, crushed

4 medium courgettes, washed and sliced in rings

1 medium green pepper, de-seeded and chopped

6oz (175g) small button mushrooms, washed and sliced

4 good size tomatoes, each cut into 8 pieces

1 bay leaf

1 level teaspoon (5ml) oregano

sea salt

freshly ground black pepper

8oz (225g) (dry weight) haricot beans, cooked (see page 60)

4 tablespoons (60ml) Cheddar cheese, finely grated

Heat the oil and sauté the onion and garlic until fairly soft, approximately 5 minutes. Cover the pan while frying. Add the courgettes and continue frying for a further 3 minutes. Add the green pepper and mushrooms and continue to fry for 3 minutes more, then add the chopped tomatoes, bay leaf, oregano, salt and pepper. Cook for 1 minute. Put the cooked beans in an ovenproof baking dish (not too deep) and pour over the vegetable mixture. Cover with foil and bake in the preheated oven for 30 minutes. When cooked, sprinkle with grated cheese and grill for a few minutes until lightly browned. Take care not to burn the top.

Serve with boiled pot barley (see page 46).

Red Kidney Beans

Guess what's first? Good old Chilli Bean Sauce.

Chilli Bean Sauce

Serves 4.

8oz (225g) (dry weight) red kidney beans, cooked
1 vegetable stock cube
2 medium onions, peeled and chopped
2 cloves garlic, crushed
2 tablespoons (30ml) sunflower or corn oil
1 medium green pepper, de-seeded and finely chopped

1 heaped teaspoon (10ml) cayenne pepper or chilli powder (less if preferred)
1 heaped teaspoon (10ml) paprika
freshly ground black pepper
14oz (396g) can tomatoes
2 tablespoons (30ml) tomato purée

Cook the beans (see page 61) adding the vegetable stock cube 10 minutes before the beans are cooked. Do not overcook. Sauté the onion and garlic in the oil for 7 minutes, add the green pepper and sauté for a further 3 minutes. Add the spices and black pepper. Stir in well and lastly mix in the tomatoes, tomato purée and drained beans. Simmer with the lid on for 15 minutes.

Serve with long grain Italian or Surinam rice. I serve this simple meal with fresh green salad tossed in Yoghurt Cheese Dressing (see page 114).

VARIATION
Just add 2oz (50g) of soaked soya (TVP) mince, beef flavour (see page 85 on Textured Vegetable Protein) to the sautéd onions and proceed as directed. TVP and beans go well.

Stuffed Spinach Pancakes with Kidney Beans *(illustrated overleaf)*

Serves 6.

Pancake mixture

4oz (110g) wholemeal flour, plain
½ teaspoon bicarbonate of soda (optional, but crispens the pancakes)
8fl oz (250ml) skimmed milk
1 level teaspoon (5ml) sea salt
2 large eggs
2 tablespoons (30ml) oil
8oz (225g) spinach, fresh or frozen, lightly cooked and drained
4 tablespoons (60ml) cold water (to be added after pancake mix has stood for 2 hours)

Filling

1 large onion, peeled and chopped
1 clove garlic, crushed
3 tablespoons (45ml) oil

1 green eating apple, chopped
1 large green pepper, de-seeded and chopped
1 teaspoon (5ml) oregano
1 bay leaf
1 level teaspoon (5ml) cayenne pepper
black pepper to taste
14oz (396g) can tomatoes
1 tablespoon (15ml) tomato purée
1 tablespoon (15ml) shoyu (naturally fermented soy sauce)
8oz (225g) (dry weight) kidney beans, cooked and drained (see page 61)
1 teacup cooking liquid from the beans
5oz (150g) Cheddar cheese, grated

Liquidise the flour, bicarbonate of soda, milk, sea salt, eggs and oil for 1 minute. (If you have no liquidiser, just add the flour gradually into the whisked eggs, milk and oil — a balloon whisk is great for this.) Then add the cold, cooked spinach and liquidise for 1 minute. (Again, if you have no liquidiser just chop the spinach up finely and mix it into the thin batter.) Leave to stand for 2 hours — it will thicken considerably — then add the cold water and stir well. To make the pancakes, brush a small, thick frying pan with oil and heat well. Place 2 tablespoons (30ml) only of the batter into the pan, turning down the heat as you do this. Spread the batter with the back of the spoon until it is thin. Take care not to press with the spoon. When the batter is spread out turn up the heat and cook for 1 minute. Shake the pancake a little to loosen it, turn it over with a fish slice and cook for ½ minute. Turn out on to a plate. Stack the pancakes on top of each other. They will not stick. Makes 9 to 10 pancakes.

Set the oven to 400°F, 200°C, Gas Mark 6. Sauté the onions and garlic in the oil for 7 minutes, add the apple and green pepper and sauté for 3 minutes. Stir in the oregano, bay leaf, cayenne pepper and black pepper. Finally add the tomatoes, tomato purée and shoyu. Stir well and simmer for 20 minutes. Take out half the sauce mix and add to the cooked, drained beans — this should be enough for 10 pancakes. Fill the pancakes and roll them up. It is easier to roll one after another in the dish you intend to bake them in. Add about ⅔ of a teacup of the reserved cooking liquid to the remaining sauce, liquidise to a pouring consistency — not too thin — and pour over the stuffed pancakes. Sprinkle on the cheese. Bake for 25 minutes until the cheese is golden brown.

After all that bother it has just got to taste good — don't worry, it does! You can make the pancakes the day before or freeze them for when you are in the mood to bake this dish. Just defrost and peel off each one.

Mung Beans

Mung Bean or Aduki Bean Shepherd's Pie

You will need a casserole dish without a lid. In this recipe I have used beef flavoured soya mince (TVP) as this gives the nearest taste to traditional shepherd's pie. In certain recipes it is invaluable, tasty, economical and highly nutritious.

Set the oven to 375°F, 190°C, Gas Mark 5.

Serves 4.

2oz (50g) soya mince (TVP), beef flavoured
6oz (175g) (dry weight) mung beans or **aduki beans, cooked (see pages 57 and 61)**
oil for frying
1 large onion, peeled and finely chopped
2 large carrots, scrubbed and finely diced (approx 6oz (175g))
3 sticks celery, finely chopped
1 clove garlic, crushed
2 tablespoons (30ml) parsley, chopped
1 bay leaf

1 teaspoon (5ml) basil
freshly ground black pepper and sea salt to taste
14oz (396g) can tomatoes, chopped
1 tablespoon (15ml) tomato purée
1 tablespoon (15ml) shoyu (naturally fermented soy sauce)
2lb (1kg) potatoes, steamed in jackets, peeled and mashed
2 tablespoons (30ml) natural yoghurt
2oz (50g) Cheddar cheese, grated
1 tomato, thinly sliced for topping

Soak the soya mince for 5 minutes in enough boiling water to just cover. Cook the mung beans and leave about ¾ cup of the cooking liquid in with them. Sauté the onion and diced carrot for 5 minutes, then add the celery and sauté for another 5 minutes. Add the garlic, parsley, bay leaf, basil, pepper, tomatoes and tomato purée and stir well. Add the shoyu and soaked mince and simmer for 5 minutes more, then mix all the ingredients together. Place the mixture in a casserole dish, top with the mashed potatoes mixed with the yoghurt and a little sea salt and black pepper. Sprinkle the grated cheese on top and garnish with the sliced tomato. Bake for 30-35 minutes.

Pinto Beans

Pinto Bean Loaf

You will need a large sheet of aluminium foil for wrapping the loaf.

Set the oven to 375°F, 190°C, Gas Mark 5.

Serves 6.

8oz (225g) (dry weight) pinto beans, cooked (see page 61)
2 tablespoons (30ml) oil for frying
1 large onion, peeled and finely chopped
1 small green or **red pepper, de-seeded and finely chopped**
4oz (110g) small button mushrooms, washed and sliced
2 tablespoons (30ml) fresh parsley, finely chopped
½ teaspoon rosemary, finely chopped

2 tablespoons (30ml) sour cream or 1 tablespoon (15ml) yoghurt plus 1 tablespoon (15ml) thick cream
4oz (110g) hazel-nuts, fairly finely ground
2oz (50g) wholemeal breadcrumbs
1 large egg to bind
sea salt and freshly ground black pepper to taste

Topping
a little beaten egg
2 tablespoons (30ml) breadcrumbs
2 tablespoons (30ml) corn or sunflower oil

Drain the cooked beans well and mash them roughly with a potato masher. Sauté the onion for 7 minutes, add the chopped pepper and mushrooms and sauté another 2 minutes only. Add the parsley, rosemary and sour cream. Stir in gently, heat through and season with sea salt and freshly ground black pepper. Mix with the remaining ingredients, adding the egg last. Grease the foil and lay it greased side up on a baking tray. Put the mixture on the foil and form into a long loaf shape. Brush with beaten egg, sprinkle with the breadcrumbs and pour the corn or sunflower oil over the crumbs. Wrap the foil loosely over the loaf and bake for 45 minutes. Open the wrapping and let the loaf brown on top after 30 minutes cooking time.

Delicious with Brown Gravy Sauce (see page 123).

Lentils

Lentil Burgers

For this recipe you can use either red split lentils, continental green or small brown lentils. Each one has its own distinct flavour.

Makes 12.

8oz (225g) (dry weight) lentils
¾ pint (400ml) hot stock or ¾ stock cube in ¾ pint hot water
1 bay leaf
1 rounded teaspoon (7ml) coriander
1 level teaspoon (5ml) cumin
1 level teaspoon (5ml) cayenne pepper
curl of lemon rind
1 onion, peeled, finely chopped and sautéd

4oz (110g) porridge oats, lightly toasted
2 tablespoons (30ml) parsley, chopped
juice of ½ lemon (approx 1 tablespoon (15ml))
1 tablespoon (15ml) shoyu (naturally fermented soy sauce)
1 egg yolk
porridge oats for coating
oil for frying

Wash the lentils well, cover with boiling water and soak for 1 hour. Drain, then cook with the stock, bay leaf, spices and lemon rind. Bring all to the boil and bubble for 5 minutes with the lid off, then simmer for 15 minutes with the lid on, until the water is absorbed. Transfer to a bowl and cool. When the lentils are cool, mix in the remaining ingredients, form into burgers ½in (1cm) thick, dip in porridge oats and fry in a little oil for 3-4 minutes on each side until golden brown.

More recipes using lentils can be found in the lesson on Indian Cuisine (see page 96).

Lentil Bake *(illustrated opposite)*

You will need a large sheet of aluminium foil for wrapping the loaf.

Set the oven to 375°F, 190°C, Gas Mark 5.

Serves 6.

10oz (275g) red split lentils
1⅓ pints (750ml) hot stock
2 bay leaves
curl of lemon rind
1 large onion, peeled and finely chopped
4 tablespoons (60ml) oil
4oz (110g) mushrooms
1 teaspoon (5ml) ground cumin
1 teaspoon (5ml) ground coriander
2 tablespoons (30ml) parsley, finely chopped
juice of ½ lemon (approx 1 tablespoon (15ml))

1 dessertspoon (10ml) shoyu (naturally fermented soy sauce)
½ teaspoon freshly ground black pepper
2oz (50g) sunflower seeds
2oz (50g) sesame seeds
3oz (75g) porridge oats, ground up with the seeds
2 tablespoons (30ml) breadcrumbs

Soak the lentils in boiling water for 1 hour then drain. Place them in an oiled, thick saucepan with the hot stock. (If you have no stock just add a vegetable stock cube to boiling water.) Add the bay leaves and a curl of lemon. Bring to the boil and boil gently with the lid off for 5 minutes. Cover and simmer gently for another 15 minutes. The lentils will then be soft and have absorbed all the liquid. Take out the bay leaves and let the mixture cool. It will thicken as it cools. Lightly toast then grind the sunflower and sesame seeds.

Sauté the onion in 2 tablespoons (30ml) of the oil for 5 minutes, add the mushrooms and sauté for 3 minutes, stir in the cumin and coriander and sauté for 1 minute only. Add the parsley, lemon juice, shoyu and black pepper. Do not cook further. Add this mixture to the lentils and finally add the seeds and oats. Place this mixture on to a well-greased sheet of foil on a baking tray. Form into a loaf shape. Pour the remaining oil over the top and sprinkle with breadcrumbs. Loosely wrap the loaf and bake for 40 minutes. Uncover the roast 10 minutes before the end of cooking time to brown the top.

Delicious cold with salad or hot with baked jacket potatoes and Onion Sauce (see page 122), or Italian Tomato Sauce (see page 124). This recipe works very well with continental green lentils too.

LESSON 6 The Soya Bean

SHOPPING LIST

Soya beans
Miso
Tofu
Cider vinegar
Soya (TVP) chunks, beef flavour
Lasagne pasta

Herbs and Spices
Allspice
Arrowroot
Five spice (from Chinese shops)
Marjoram
Paprika pepper
Fresh ginger

The first taste I had of the soya bean should definitely have turned me off it for life. Fortunately, this wonderful little creamy bean would not lose itself in my cupboard. Every time I looked at it, I thought of the belly-aching stew I had eaten at a well-meaning friend's dinner party. Something about this first failure kept on challenging me to do better. What I had read about the nutritional value of the soya bean in books written by wholefood writers kept on niggling at my conscience, so much that I decided to experiment with this valuable source of protein. I was determined to create dishes that would be acceptable to my family and friends.

I can remember my first try at beef mince shepherd's pie. It was awful, but it only took two or three goes to make it delicious. This gave me hope. You have to use your imagination with raw meat, then why not use this imagination on its vegetable equivalent, protein-wise. Why? Well, for one good reason, the soya bean is much cheaper and it contains almost 40 per cent protein. In fact, it contains as much protein as top quality steak. Unlike meat, it contains unsaturated fat (see page 8 in the introduction) and it is very high in lecithin which reduces the level of cholesterol in the blood, thus lessening the possibility of heart attacks. As it is the most alkaline of foods it can be used to correct acidity in the system. The soya bean is the cheapest source of minerals and complete protein on the market today.

Although the body cannot manufacture the eight amino acids which are found in meat, dairy produce and the soya bean, it is now generally accepted that less complete protein sources such as beans, nuts and seeds are perfectly adequate if eaten in the right combinations. For example, if we eat beans with whole grains, we have a complete protein, if we combine nuts or seeds with whole grains, we have a complete protein — the amino acids lacking in one food are made whole with the amino acids in the other. All this I have mentioned in the notes on beans in Lesson 5 but, in fact, this point of balancing different proteins to achieve a complete protein is very important and worth reinforcing.

I have also pointed out in Lesson 5 that all raw peas and beans contain inhibitors which are harmful to the digestion. This applies even more so to the raw soya bean. In its raw state, this worthy bean contains a trypsin inhibitor which prevents the body assimilating an important amino acid called methionine. The bean, the flour from the bean and sprouted soya beans must be cooked to render these substances completely harmless.

The most important point of all is that this wonderful bean feeds so many for so little. As I said in the introduction to Lesson 5, one harvest of soya beans grown on one acre of land will provide enough protein for one person for approximately six years. In comparison with this, that very same harvest fed to animals will only supply enough protein for one human being for eighty days. Surely this, in a time of really serious economic and ecological problems, and no matter what your preference gastronomically, is a vital reason for having a go with the soya bean in all its versatility. I will try to bring some of this versatility to life for you in the recipes that are to follow.

Cooking soya beans
Wash well and pick over for little stones, as with all beans, peas and lentils. Soak in cold water three times the volume of the beans, i.e. 1 cup of beans to 3 cups of water. Change the water three times during soaking. Soak for 24 hours in a cool place. Rinse the beans well after soaking and add 3 pints (1·5 litres) of fresh water to cook the beans in. Bring to the boil, let the beans bubble for 10 minutes then simmer with a lid on for 2½-3½ hours. The time needed depends a lot on how old your beans are. A freshly dried crop will sometimes take only 2 hours but it can take as much as 4 hours.

Here are a couple of recipes to start you off with this wonder bean. The other recipes in this lesson involve using products derived from the bean.

Soya Burgers

These are delicious served in soft baps with Italian Tomato Sauce (see page 124) and salad.

Makes 8.

To make your own baps use my bread recipe (see page 13) but substitute unbleached white flour for half the wholemeal flour. Take 2oz (50g) portions of the dough, roll into slightly flattened balls and bake for 15 minutes at 450°F, 230°C, Gas Mark 8.

6oz (175g) (dry weight) soya beans
4oz (110g) porridge oats
1 onion, peeled and finely chopped
1 small green pepper, de-seeded and finely chopped (optional, but great)
1 tablespoon (15ml) parsley, finely chopped
1 tablespoon (15ml) shoyu (naturally fermented soy sauce)
1 teaspoon (5ml) basil
1 tablespoon (15ml) lemon juice
1 clove garlic, crushed
1 egg
a little sea salt and freshly ground black pepper to taste
oil for frying

Cook the beans as directed on this page. Drain and mash with a potato masher. Add all the other ingredients. The mixture should be reasonably stiff but not too dry. Form into balls slightly bigger than a golf ball and flatten to just under ½in (1cm) thick. Fry in hot oil ¼in (0·5cm) deep. When golden brown on one side, pop them over with a fish slice to brown on the other.

Barbecued Soya Beans

Serves 6.

12oz (350g) (dry weight) soya beans
4 tablespoons (60ml) oil
2 medium onions, peeled and finely
  chopped
2 large cloves garlic, crushed
1 level teaspoon (5ml) allspice
1 level teaspoon (5ml) cayenne
  pepper
1 level teaspoon (5ml) paprika
  pepper

4 tablespoons (60ml) tomato purée
14oz (396g) can tomatoes
1 teacup apple juice
4 tablespoons (60ml) soft dark
  sugar
4 tablespoons (60ml) lemon juice
dash of Tabasco sauce
2 tablespoons (30ml) shoyu
  (naturally fermented soy sauce)

Cook the soya beans as directed on page 77 and drain. Sauté the onion and garlic in the oil for 10 minutes until soft but not browned. Add the spices and stir into the onion, then add all the other ingredients except the shoyu and stir well together. Bring to the boil then reduce heat to simmer and cook for 15 minutes. Add the drained soya beans and shoyu. Simmer gently on a low heat for another 20 minutes with the lid on. If the sauce is too thick just add a little more apple juice. Lovely on wholemeal toast for a snack or with baked jacket potatoes and salad as a main meal.

Soya Bean Products

SOYA FLOUR. Soya bean flour has even greater nutritional value than the beans. It is highly concentrated and contains no gluten, so it is great for those on a gluten-free diet. It makes marvellous creamy white sauce and is a useful and healthy thickener for soups and stews. As well as thickening, it adds concentrated protein. I sometimes add it to my flour when bread making (see page 14 — Bread with a Different Flavour). For achieving a really smooth, creamy savoury sauce see page 122.

SHOYU AND TAMARI (naturally fermented soy sauce). There are many brands of soy sauce on the market. Most are synthetically compounded with additives such as caramel and syrup to give colour and flavour. These products are to be avoided; although they are cheaper to manufacture and, in fact, are made within a few days, they do not produce the protein yield of the naturally fermented soy sauces, shoyu and tamari.

Traditionally, the method of producing the natural sauce is to ferment the beans in vats with water, roasted cracked wheat and natural salt for one to three years. This fermentation process produces a source of vitamin B_{12}, the one vitamin which is thought to be non-existent in a diet of plants alone. Further, the combination of grains with soya beans increases the protein yield, while the fermentation process itself enables our bodies to utilise the protein more efficiently. Added to this, when the natural sauce is added to other foods such as whole grains, nuts, seeds and beans, it increases the amount of protein that can be digested.

MISO. A wonder food! I don't say that flippantly, because just two good teaspoons (10ml) of miso will give you enough complete protein for one day. How about that! So many of our fellow humans starve and the answer to feeding the poor millions need not be so very difficult.

Miso is a soya bean paste produced by lactic fermentation. The process is lengthy, during which a culture is added to cooked soya beans and cooked rice. Salt is gradually added until the mixture achieves a paste-like consistency. The paste comes in various shades. The darker miso contains up to 90 per cent soya bean while the lighter miso contains more rice and thus less protein. Not only is miso a high protein food but it is also free of cholesterol; it is an aid to digestion, is claimed to help develop a strong resistance to disease and, the most incredible claim of all, which has been substantiated, is that it can remove radioactive substances from the body.

Cooking with miso
Don't cook it, or at least only let it simmer for one minute in your soup or casserole. Cooking destroys the culture and flavour. Also very important is not just to dollop a lump of miso into your prepared meal. Mix the miso with a little of the hot stock or some warm water to a smooth paste, then stir this with a fork into the prepared food. Remember that miso is salty and it is not necessary to include salt in any dish to which you will be adding miso.

How do *I* use miso? Well, I have found miso a fantastic tonic. Cook or no cook, and I am one of those people who feels somehow they must feed the world around them — meaning anyone who is there at any time, but I do have off days when I just do not want to prepare anything. Here's my recipe for a good quick tonic.

Simple Miso Tonic

Liquidise two grated carrots in 7fl oz (200ml) of hot water and stir in one good teaspoon (5ml) of miso. Your body will feel better within minutes. That is my experience. Take the tonic twice daily — very simple and enough for those off-days.

Other recipes for miso are not necessary because I simply use it as an extra protein booster and always in vegetable soups or less complete protein bean stews. When I say vegetable soups, I mean hearty soups such as root vegetable, not leek soup or asparagus, as miso is strong tasting and would destroy the delicate flavour of such vegetables.

SOYA MILK. Soya milk is richer in iron than cows' milk but is lower in calcium, phosphorus and vitamin A. It is invaluable for those who suffer from allergies related to cows' milk. It is rich in linoleic acid and lecithin, both of which have been proved to reduce the level of cholesterol in the blood.

Soya milk is nutritionally similar to breast milk and is suitable for children who cannot digest cows' milk properly. It is easy to obtain in wholefood shops and health stores. Plamil, which is available in tins, is specially fortified to suit the needs of babies. Soya milk is also very simple to make.

TOFU (SOYA CHEESE). Tofu is a high protein food, easily digested, cholesterol-free and low in calories. It has more protein relative to calories than any other food. It can be substituted for cottage cheese in any recipe.

So bland and yet so rich, wholesome and precious a food, but it has taken me so long to really make tofu a part of my daily diet. It reminded me of junket, which I hated as a child and I avoided it for years. But the more I read about wholefoods, the more this valuable source of protein kept nagging me to understand its wonderful value. What was I to do but make it for myself and experiment with my own home-made soya cheese. I made the cheese and left it in the fridge for three days without a glimmer of an inspiration. Then my obstinacy evaporated and I took that piece of bean curd and made it into a fantastic spread. That was just the beginning. My recipes for tofu are also only a beginning. Its uses are endless. I hope my choice will encourage you to experiment with this wonderful food.

To make Soya Milk and Tofu (Soya Cheese)

Read all the instructions carefully and have everything ready before you start. The whole process is illustrated on pages 82 and 83.

You can make tofu with Epsom salts or lemon juice, but I find the best results – a higher yield and greater firmness – are achieved by using Nigari. Nigari is rich in minerals and is the residue left after the salt (sodium chloride) and water are removed from sea water. The residue is sun-dried and bought as crystals.

I also use a Japanese tofu press which is made from Japanese cypress wood (iroki). Both Nigari and the tofu press can be obtained by mail order from the address on page 158. The press comes with a sachet of Nigari and full instructions, but it is best to follow my instructions as they give you the exact amount of water to use, which is most important. The quantities given make 1lb (450g) of firm tofu.

12oz (350g) (dry weight) soya beans
2 teaspoons (10ml) Nigari, dissolved in 1 teacup of warm water or
3 teaspoons (15ml) Epsom salts, dissolved in 1 teacup of warm water

or **6 tablespoons (90ml) lemon juice in 1 cup of warm water (this will give you a tangy, slightly coarse tofu, which is quite tasty)**

To make the Soya Milk

Wash the soya beans and soak for 24 hours. Change the water three times during soaking. Rinse the beans well after soaking and to each cup of soaked beans add 1 cup of boiling water and liquidise cup by cup. Leave the motor on for 1½ minutes each time to achieve a reasonably smooth, runny batter consistency. Grease a large, heavy-bottomed pan big enough to take about 10 pints (5 litres) of liquid. Bring 8 cups of fresh water to the boil and pour in the liquidised bean purée. Bring to the boil, stirring constantly. Keep on a moderate heat only, to prevent burning. Once boiling, turn down the heat and leave to simmer for 20 minutes. The mixture will be frothy so spoon back some of the froth to make sure that the liquid is gently bubbling underneath. Stir occasionally.

Dissolve the Nigari in the water (or the Epsom salts or lemon juice) to make your solidifier. Stretch a straining bag or good sized piece of muslin over a colander, leaving plenty for tying up. Place the colander over a large clean bowl to catch the milk. Put on rubber gloves and pour the boiled bean liquid into the straining bag or muslin. The soya milk will filter through. Rinse the cooking pot with 1 cup of boiling water and add this to the straining bag. Twist the bag or cloth tightly and squeeze out as much milk as possible. Open the bag and pour in three more cups of boiling water, tie up and squeeze again. The soya milk is now ready.

The milk will freeze well after it is cooled. The quicker you cool the milk, the longer it will keep, so if you don't want to make tofu, cool it by immersing the bowl in a sink of cold water, changing the water as it warms. Soya milk will keep fresh in the fridge for up to 4 days. Frozen, it will be good for 3 months at least. You can use soya milk in any recipe requiring cows' milk, especially in sauces.

To make Tofu (Soya Cheese) Rinse out the cooking pot, pour the hot soya milk back into it and reheat. The milk must reach at least 185°F, so bring it to just under boiling point. (*Note:* if using Epsom salts, 165°F is hot enough). After it is hot, remove from the cooker and add your chosen solidifier by stirring briskly and *slowly* pouring in one-third of the Nigari, Epsom salts or lemon juice liquid. Continue to stir for half a minute, making sure you stir in milk from the sides and bottom of the pan. Let the movement of the liquid stop then using the back of your stirring spoon, pour a further third of the solidifier on to the surface of the milk. *Cover* and leave for 3 minutes, then stir again. Using the back of the spoon trickle the remaining solidifier over the surface of the milk, then slowly and gently stir only a half inch (about one centimetre) of the surface of the milk as you count up to twenty. Cover and leave for another 3 minutes, then uncover and stir the liquid. You should now have a mixture of curds and whey. The curds will be cream-coloured and the whey a clear yellow colour. Line the tofu press with a clean piece of muslin, draping it over the edge as it will be folded over the tofu later. If you have no press just place the cloth over a colander which is on top of a bowl, to catch the whey. Ladle the curds and whey into the press or colander. The curds will stay in the cloth and the whey will drip through. The tofu will be quite soft at this stage. Fold the cloth over the tofu, place the lid of the press on top (or a small plate if you are using a colander) and weight on top of this. The weight should be about 2lb (1kg). Leave to stand for 20-30 minutes. This will give you a firm tofu which is easy to slice. Uncover the tofu. To keep in the refrigerator, fill a bowl with cold water and ease the tofu into this. Change the water every day and it will last in the fridge for 6 days. You can freeze it but the texture alters and it is then only good for soups and stews.

Tofu is available commercially in vacuum packs weighing 10½oz (297g) but this is soft and not easy to use in recipes. You can press it and leave it to drip, which will make it firmer, but you will end up with a very small amount of tofu, so it is not worthwhile. Although it seems a lengthy process, home-made tofu is well worth the effort.

What to do with the pulp left over after making the soya milk? This is known as *okara*. It is 3.5 per cent protein and a good fibre to add to your breakfast cereal. Here is a super, tasty recipe using okara, jam-packed with goodness, and it can be stored.

1. Liquidising the soya beans
with boiling water.

2. Transferring the soya purée to
a large cooking pot.

3. Pouring the boiled bean liquid
into a muslin-lined colander.

4. Squeezing out as much soya
milk as possible.

5. Adding the chosen solidifier

6. Ladling the curd mixture into the tofu press.

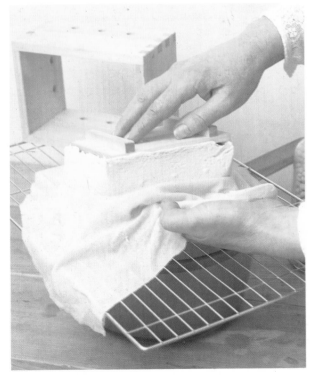

7. Removing the tofu from the press.

8. Placing the square of tofu in fresh, cold water.

Toasted Okara Muesli Breakfast

Makes about 3¼ lb (1·5kg).

2 large mugs (capacity 1 pint (450ml)) okara
1 large cup (capacity ½ pint (275ml)) porridge oats
3 generous tablespoons (60ml) malt extract
3 tablespoons (45ml) clear honey
2 tablespoons (45ml) sunflower oil

2oz (50g) sesame seeds
2oz (50g) sunflower seeds
2oz (50g) chopped hazel-nuts or almonds
good pinch sea salt
6oz (175g) raisins or dried apricots, chopped

To dry the okara just spread it on a large baking tray and place in the oven at 300°F, 150°C, Gas Mark 2, and stir it occasionally. Do not brown, just let it dry.

Place the dry okara with all the other ingredients, *except* the raisins or apricots, in a large, thick saucepan. Toast the mixture over a medium heat, stirring constantly to prevent burning, until it is crisp and golden brown. Let it cool. Stir in the dried fruit and put into a storage jar. A truly healthy treat eaten with milk or yoghurt at any time of the day, especially at breakfast time.

Sweet and Sour Tofu *(illustrated on page 86)*

Really a beautiful dish. Colourful, tasty and authentic in taste.

Serves 4.

Sauce
4 tablespoons (60ml) sesame seed or safflower oil for frying
1 medium onion, peeled and finely chopped
1 large carrot, scrubbed and thinly sliced
2 cloves garlic, crushed
2oz (50g) bean sprouts
2oz (50g) button mushrooms, washed and sliced
1 green pepper, de-seeded and finely chopped
1 heaped teaspoon (10ml) fresh ginger, grated
1 teaspoon (5ml) five spice (see shopping list, page 76) or allspice
2oz (50g) dried peaches, soaked in 1½ cups (about ½ pint (275ml)) apple juice overnight, cooked for 15 minutes and chopped, reserving the juice and making up to ½ pint (275ml) with cold water

2 tablespoons (30ml) tomato purée
3 tablespoons (45ml) cider vinegar
3 tablespoons (45ml) soft dark sugar
2 tablespoons (30ml) shoyu (naturally fermented soy sauce)
1 good tablespoon (20ml) arrowroot or cornflour

Tofu
10oz (275g) piece tofu, home-made or bought
½ cup wholemeal flour
sea salt and black pepper to taste
pinch garlic powder
1 teaspoon (5ml) basil or oregano
shoyu for coating
oil for semi-deep frying

To make the sauce, sauté the onion, carrot and garlic in the oil for 5 minutes. Add the bean sprouts, mushrooms and green pepper and sauté for another 3 minutes. Add the ginger and five spice and stir well into the vegetables, then add all the remaining ingredients except the arrowroot or cornflour. Stir the mixture over a gentle heat. Mix the arrowroot or cornflour with 2 tablespoons (30ml) of cold water, bring the sauce to the boil and add the arrowroot mixture. Stir all the time while it thickens.

Chop the tofu slices into rectangular slices approximately ½in (1cm) thick and 1in (2·5cm) long. Mix the flour, sea salt, pepper, garlic powder and basil together. Dip the tofu in a saucer of shoyu, then in the flour mixture and semi-deep fry in hot oil until golden brown. Tricky the first time you do this, but well worth getting the knack.

To serve this tasty and highly nutritious dish I put the cooked tofu in the centre of a bed of Surinam rice (see page 44) then pour over the sweet and sour vegetable sauce. Surround the dish with sprigs of watercress and see how pleasing it is to the eye.

Simple Deep Fried Tofu *(illustrated on page 86)*

Chop the required amount of tofu into rectangular slices approximately ¾in (2cm) thick and 2in (5cm) long. Soak in shoyu for a few minutes then drain on a piece of cloth. Cover with another piece of cloth or kitchen paper for a few minutes to absorb the excess moisture then deep fry until crisp and golden brown. Delicious and a protein booster for simple meatless spaghetti sauces.

The recipes in which you can use tofu are endless. For example, to make a simple spread for luncheon toasties, just add a little garlic, mixed herbs, cayenne pepper and a little sea salt to the tofu. Sandwich this mixture between wholemeal toast slices, plus a little green salad wedged in and you will have a very wholesome lunch. So get cracking and experiment with tofu, it deserves your imagination.

TEXTURED VEGETABLE PROTEIN. This is a very misused product of the soya bean. I have tasted some awful meals with TVP in some form or another used as the main ingredient. I avoided it for years but the more I read about its value, both nutritionally and economically (5oz (150g) TVP is equal to 1lb (450g) lean beef steak), I gradually found myself experimenting with it. When you look at the price difference you will see why I just had to succeed in cooking with this valuable food. Not only has it the advantage of being cheap to produce and consequently inexpensive to buy, but it is also cholesterol-free. After many failures, I at last succeeded in producing meals that were not just acceptable but greatly enjoyed by my students, friends and family. As I have said before, food has to taste good and not just be good for you.

Although there are many varieties of specially flavoured textured vegetable proteins on the market, I am going to stick to TVP mince and TVP chunks, both beef-flavoured, as these are the ones I find most popular and a good starting point. I hope these recipes and ideas on how to use TVP in a variety of ways prove as successful with your family as they are with mine.

Opposite Bolognese Sauce.

Right Simple Deep Fried Tofu (see page 85).

Below Sweet and Sour Tofu (see page 84).

Bolognese Sauce *(illustrated opposite)*

I usually make a good lot of this sauce at once and any leftovers I add to rice to make a simple risotto topped with grated cheese for the following day's lunch or supper.

3oz (75g) soya (TVP) mince, beef flavour

2 medium onions or 1 large Spanish onion, peeled and finely chopped

1 clove garlic, crushed

3 tablespoons (45ml) olive oil for frying

4 sticks celery, finely chopped

1 green pepper, de-seeded and chopped

4oz (110g) small button mushrooms, washed and sliced (optional)

2 tablespoons (30ml) fresh parsley, chopped

1 heaped teaspoon (10ml) basil

½ teaspoon marjoram

2 bay leaves

2oz (50g) hazel, almond or cashew nuts, roughly ground (optional)

1lb 12oz (794g) can tomatoes, chopped

2 tablespoons (30ml) tomato purée

freshly ground black pepper to taste (approx ½ teaspoon)

sea salt to taste or 1 vegetable stock cube

1 tablespoon (15ml) lemon juice (optional, but seems to enhance the flavour)

Reconstitute the soya mince by just covering it with hot water and leave to swell for 10 minutes. Sauté the onion and garlic in the oil for 5 minutes, add the celery and sauté for another 5 minutes. Add the green pepper and mushrooms and continue frying for another 3 minutes. Stir in the parsley, basil, marjoram and bay leaves. At this stage add the reconstituted soya mince. Stir it into the vegetables for 2 minutes so that it absorbs the flavour. This is important. Add the nuts and finally the tomatoes, tomato purée, pepper and sea salt or stock cube. Mix all the ingredients together well and simmer for 35 minutes. Taste and add the lemon juice if you wish.

I serve this with either buckwheat spaghetti (see notes on buckwheat on page 45), wholemeal spaghetti or wholemeal spaghetti rings. Top this with either freshly grated Parmesan cheese (never packet grated — it can ruin a meal) or grated farmhouse Cheddar. All this for a quarter of the usual price of the same quantity of meat and you will never know the difference. Have a go!

For a good tasty shepherd's pie recipe using soya mince see page 72. Mung Bean Shepherd's Pie is always a firm favourite.

Soya Chunk Steak Pie

Whatever your opinion of soya chunks, this tastes great! You will need a 10in (25cm) pie dish.

Set the oven to 375°F, 190°C, Gas Mark 5.

Serves 5.

4oz (110g) soya (TVP) chunks, beef flavour
1 medium onion, peeled and chopped
1 clove garlic, crushed (optional)
2 carrots, scrubbed and cut into thin, 1in (2·5cm) sticks
3 tablespoons (45ml) sunflower oil
3 sticks celery, chopped
1 leek, cleaned and chopped
½ green pepper, de-seeded and chopped
1 tablespoon (15ml) fresh parsley, chopped

1 teaspoon (5ml) mixed herbs
1 tablespoon (15ml) wholemeal flour or unbleached white flour
½ stock cube
1 generous tablespoon (20ml) tomato purée
1 tablespoon (15ml) shoyu (naturally fermented soy sauce) (optional)
8oz (225g) basic wholemeal cheese pastry (see page 18)
beaten egg and water mixture or milk, to glaze

Soak the soya chunks in 1 pint (550ml) of boiling water for 2 hours. (The water in which you have previously boiled one chopped onion is great. Strain, and pour the boiling liquid over the soya chunks.) Do not add salt.

Sauté the onion, garlic and carrots in the oil for 5 minutes. Add the celery and leeks and continue frying for 3 minutes. Drain the soya chunks, reserving the liquid, and add them, with the green pepper, parsley and mixed herbs. Sauté for 2 minutes more. Add the flour and stir into the mixture for 1 minute. Add the ½ stock cube and enough hot water to make the reserved soaking liquid up to 1 pint (550ml) and stir this with the tomato purée into the vegetables and soya chunks. Cook on a low heat for 15 minutes. Taste and add the shoyu if you wish for extra flavour and colour. Pour the mixture into the pie dish and leave to cool. When cold, roll out the pastry and place on top, seal the edges and crimp. Brush with beaten egg and water mixture or milk, to glaze. Bake for 30 minutes.

Goulash

Very simple and quick to make.

Serves 4.

4oz (110g) soya (TVP) chunks, beef flavour
1 large Spanish onion or 2 medium onions, peeled and chopped
1 large clove garlic, crushed
3 tablespoons (45ml) sunflower oil
1 large green pepper, de-seeded and chopped
1 bay leaf
1 vegetable or meat stock cube or ½ teaspoon (2·5ml) sea salt

freshly ground black pepper
2 tablespoons (30ml) paprika
1 level tablespoon (15ml) wholemeal flour
1 tablespoon (15ml) tomato purée
1lb 12oz (794g) can tomatoes, chopped
5oz (150g) natural yoghurt, mixed with 1 tablespoon (15ml) thick cream

Reconstitute the soya chunks by soaking them for 2 hours in enough hot water to cover them by 1in (2·5cm). Make sure that they remain covered with water during the soaking time. Drain them well after soaking. Sauté the onion and garlic in the oil for 10 minutes. Add the green pepper and continue sautéing for another 3 minutes. Add the bay leaf, stock cube or sea salt, black pepper and paprika. Stir in well and then add the soya chunks. Fry the whole mixture gently for at least 2 minutes. Stir in the flour, then add the tomato purée and tomatoes. Mix well together and simmer for 45 minutes to 1 hour. When cooked and just before serving, stir in the yoghurt and cream mixture.

Serve with long grain brown rice and salad or steamed green vegetables. My children loved this right from the start. It was my first effort using soya chunks.

Finally, just a few hints on using TVP in other main dishes.

Stuffed Marrow

This is absolutely delicious with leftover Bolognese Sauce equally mixed, in weight, with cooked brown rice. I slice the marrow in rings 1in (2·5cm) thick, remove the seeds and core from each and stuff with the rice mixture. I then top this with a cheese sauce (see page 122), sprinkle grated farmhouse Cheddar cheese and mixed herbs over this and bake in the oven at 350°F, 180°C, Gas Mark 4, for at least 1 hour, or until the marrow is soft.

If you want to do this a quicker way, just steam the hollowed-out marrow rings for 15 minutes before filling them. This will cut the oven baking time by half. If you do the quick baking method, set the oven to 400°F, 200°C, Gas Mark 6 and bake for 30 minutes until golden brown on top.

Italian Lasagne

For this, I use the basic Bolognese Sauce, sautéing the vegetables with olive oil and adding 1 small glass of red table wine (optional) to the sauce. I find that the pre-cooked green (spinach) lasagne pasta, which is made from whole durum wheat, is great for this recipe. Just line a large, 3in (7·5cm) deep, square or rectangular baking dish with the pasta, spoon on the Bolognese sauce and dot with curd cheese, cottage cheese or tofu. Place another layer of pasta on top of this and again dot with the soft cheese. Cover this with another layer of pasta. Top with cheese sauce (see page 122). Sprinkle on freshly grated Parmesan cheese (not the packed grated variety) or grated farmhouse Cheddar. Over this put a little basil or oregano and bake for 1 hour at 350°F, 180°C, Gas Mark 4. This has never failed to please anyone who has tasted the recipe in my classes or among our friends and family.

There are many more ways of using the soya bean and the products derived from it but I sincerely hope that this lesson and my choice of recipes will inspire you to experiment for yourself with this valuable and economical source of complete protein.

LESSON 7

Nuts and Seeds

ALMONDS
PUMPKIN SEEDS
WALNUTS

SHOPPING LIST

You will possibly have a reasonable supply of nuts and seeds already, as I have included these items in many recipes throughout the lessons. However, the list will include some of those ingredients already mentioned as you will probably need to replenish your stocks by now

Almonds
Cashew nuts
Hazel nuts
Sesame seeds
Sunflower seeds

Pumpkin seeds
Dates
Raisins
Dried apricots

Nuts

Nuts are a high protein food rich in the B vitamins and minerals and well worth making a regular ingredient in your diet. Although they have a high fat content, they are rich in linoleic acid which helps control the level of cholesterol.

The majority of us, me included in the past, eat nuts only at Christmas or with drinks. Well, the Christmas nuts eaten straight from the shells are great but the packeted variety really should be avoided. They are often treated with preservatives, colourings and other inhibitors and roasted in saturated fats, which causes problems to our digestive system. You can, however, obtain a good variety of assorted unshelled and unsalted nuts all year round from wholefood or health food shops, where the turnover is higher for this particular food than in supermarkets. This is important because they do not have a long shelf life. They become soft and rancid tasting if stored for too long.

Seeds

I love them and add them to as many dishes as I can. Bursting with goodness, they are a wonderful, easily digested source of vitamins and minerals, and very high in linoleic acid. Little did I know a few years back, when showering our gerbils with those small, stripey sunflower seeds, what a precious food I was missing. Now they are, thankfully, a regular ingredient in my everyday recipes.

The list of nuts and seeds which is to follow will, I hope, give you enough information as to their nutritional value to encourage you to seek fresh supplies and incorporate them into your daily eating habits.

CASHEWS HAZEL-NUTS PECAN NUTS
SESAME SEEDS SUNFLOWER SEEDS
PINE NUTS (OR KERNELS) BRAZIL NUTS PISTACHIO NUTS

ALMONDS. These delicately flavoured nuts impart a delicious flavour to both savoury and sweet dishes alike. Almond oil was one of the earliest skin beautifiers and is still used today in many face creams. In the Middle East and India, almonds are a common ingredient in delicious savoury rice dishes and in sweet making. Almond paste (marzipan) is very popular spread on cakes at festive times. Try using fruit sugar with almonds when next you are making marzipan. I often add these nuts to stir-fry vegetables and sweet and sour sauce dishes.

BRAZIL NUTS. I was amazed the first time I saw a picture of these nuts growing on a tree. What you see growing are large, coconut-type shells jam packed inside with brazil nuts as we know them. They are 33% protein and are high in linoleic acid, but have a very high calorific content so are to be avoided if your are on a slimming diet.

CASHEW NUTS. Everyone seems to like cashews. Like almonds, they impart a lovely, mild flavour when lightly toasted and added to savoury rice dishes. A native of Brazil, the cashew nut grows on the end of a pear-shaped fruit, which is often eaten by the Brazilians, the nut itself being discarded.

HAZEL-NUTS. These nuts are absolutely invaluable in sweet dishes. They go under various names such as cob-nuts and filberts, depending on their country of origin. I use them often in cakes and biscuits, toasted and chopped in my breakfast muesli or sprinkled over ice cream.

PECAN NUTS. The shelled pecan nut looks very similar in shape to the walnut. It is reddish in colour and I think has a much nicer flavour than the slightly bitter-tasting walnut. In America, they are called hickory nuts. I love them in rich fruit cakes and as a change from chopped almonds. Another idea is to rub a little cinnamon and nutmeg into chopped pecans, sprinkle them on top of an egg custard flan before baking and see what a delicious sweet results.

PINE NUTS or KERNELS. These tiny, cream-coloured nuts grow inside the hard cones of the stone pine tree and are a very popular ingredient in Mediterranean cuisine (see the recipe for Stuffed Spinach Leaves on page 49). I often add them to sweet and sour sauce or lightly toast them and sprinkle over a vegetable curry with rice. They are, unfortunately, quite expensive but a few go a long way flavour-wise.

PISTACHIO NUTS. These are my favourite nuts, but very highly priced. I remember one Christmas I was given a present of a box of freshly shelled, unsalted pistachios, and I will never forget the taste of that Christmas nut roast or the pistachio ice cream. Their superb flavour enriches any sweet or savoury dish they are put into.

WALNUTS. Walnuts vary in flavour and can sometimes be very bitter, so nibble one or two before you add them to a particular dish. I like them chopped up in a salad with apples and Chinese leaves. I also find they go well with bananas as in the Banana and Walnut Cake on page 30.

PUMPKIN SEEDS. These seeds, which are either light or dark green in colour, are richer in iron than any other seed. They are 30% protein, high in phosphorus, a good source of vitamin B and rich in unsaturated fatty acids. They have a pleasant, distinctive flavour and are well worth getting to know as an ingredient in your cooking. Tests have revealed that these seeds seem to be a powerful healing aid in cases of bladder disorder.

SESAME SEEDS. I'm a sesame seed addict. I throw them into any recipe I can — bread, cakes or biscuits, and I coat rissoles with them. They are a good source of protein, vitamins and minerals. A great calcium booster. *Tahini* is a marvellous paste made from ground sesame seeds with added sesame seed oil. It is a common ingredient in Greek and Middle Eastern cooking (see Falafal on page 65 and Hummous on page 128).

SUNFLOWER SEEDS. Sunflower seeds are not just for tiny caged animals. We deserve them as well. The seeds are very high in linoleic acid, contain approximately 25% protein, are a rich source of vitamins B and E and are well supplied with important minerals. Mix them into your breakfast cereals, toast them and fork them into savoury rice or bulgur salad or fresh salads. To make a tasty spread, highly charged nutritionally, try making my Sunflower Seed and Honey Butter (see page 95).

You will find many recipes scattered throughout the book using nuts and seeds but I have selected only a few especially for this lesson that have nuts and seeds as main ingredients. I will start with a nut roast which I have found to be a most enjoyable and well-received alternative to the traditional meat roast.

Nut Roast

You will need a large roasting tin and a 6 x 12in (15 x 30cm) piece of aluminium foil to cap the roast.

Set the oven to 375°F, 190°C, Gas Mark 5.

Serves 6.

12oz (350g) mixed nuts and seeds (equal amounts of cashews, hazels, almonds and sunflower seeds make a good combination)
6oz (175g) wholemeal breadcrumbs
1 medium onion, peeled and finely chopped (approx 6oz (175g))

3 tablespoons (45ml) fresh parsley, chopped
2 tablespoons (30ml) shoyu (naturally fermented soy sauce)
3 tablespoons (75ml) cold pressed sunflower oil
2 eggs, medium size
1oz (25g) pumpkin seeds

Grind the nuts and seeds so that they look like medium-fine crumbs — not too powdery. Mix all the ingredients together, (saving the pumpkin seeds and 2 tablespoons (30ml) of oil for the top), and squeeze with your hands. Oil the roasting tin well and form the mixture into a loaf shape in the tin. Pour the reserved oil over the top and sprinkle with the pumpkin seeds. Cap this loosely with the foil and bake for 45 minutes.

I serve this with roast potatoes (steam in their jackets for 15 minutes, peel the thin skins off, place them around the roast and pour a little oil over each) baked carrots, any lightly steamed green vegetables in season and a simple Brown Gravy Sauce (see page 123 for this recipe).

Nut Rissoles

Makes 8.

Using the same basic ingredients as in the Nut Roast recipe, but varying the choice of nuts and seeds, I add 1 teaspoon (5ml) tarragon and form the mixture into rissoles ½in (1cm) thick (weight of each 3oz (75g)). Dip the rissoles in sesame seeds and fry in oil ¼in (0·5cm) deep over moderate heat for 4 minutes on each side. Do not over-cook or cook them too quickly as they will dry out. Delicious served with Mushroom Sauce (see page 123), jacket potatoes and salad or just with chutney and salad.

Nutty Paté *(illustrated above)*

Delicious in pitta bread (see page 13), in sandwiches or just as a dip.

3 cups mixed nuts and seeds (my choice is almonds, hazels, cashews, sesame seeds and sunflower seeds)

6 tablespoons (90ml) cold pressed sunflower or safflower oil

6 tablespoons (90ml) natural yoghurt

1 tablespoon (15ml) shoyu (naturally fermented soy sauce)

1 small onion, peeled and very finely chopped or 1 small bunch of spring onions, chopped (use all green parts)

1 teaspoon (5ml) mixed herbs

a little chopped red or green pepper

a little fresh ground black pepper

All you do is toast the nuts in a thick, dry saucepan over a medium heat, stirring constantly with a wooden spoon for about 6 minutes. Grind the nuts in a liquidiser until powdery, then put all the ingredients in a bowl and mix them together.

This paté spread on hot pitta bread with salad makes a truly fabulous meal for lunch or supper.

Fruit and Nut Sausage.

Sunflower Seed and Honey Butter

This recipe is very simple and the choice of how sweet to make it is up to you.

Toast some sunflower seeds in a thick, dry pan for just 5 minutes, stirring constantly. Liquidise the seeds to a powdery consistency, put into a bowl and mix with clear honey to a smooth paste. You can use equal amounts of sunflower and sesame seeds for this recipe. It makes a very nutritious spread on wholemeal toast for children.

Tahini and Shoyu Spread

Another very simple sandwich filler. To 1 tablespoon (15ml) tahini add a few drops of shoyu, mix well and there you are. Adding salad to the sandwich only makes it more delicious. A little garlic in the spread is worth a try.

Fruit and Nut Sausage *(illustrated above)*

This recipe was given to me by our local home brew wine maker, Mr John Jackson. His wine is equally delightful. The recipe originated from his mother. I have added apricots and sesame seeds to the original recipe but it seems to taste good with any fruit and nut mixture.

8oz (225g) dates
4oz (110g) dried apricots, well washed
8oz (225g) raisins

8oz (225g) mixed nuts and sunflower seeds
a few toasted sesame seeds for coating

Steam the dates and apricots for 20 minutes in a colander, putting the apricots at the bottom. Put all the ingredients except the sesame seeds through a mincer, then knead the mixture well together for 1 minute. Roll into a sausage shape or cut into finger slices and coat with sesame seeds, pressing the seeds firmly into the mixture. Naturally sweet and full of goodness!

LESSON 8 Indian Cuisine

SHOPPING LIST

Most of the spices are available from Indian shops. Again, you will probably have collected a good supply of spices as you have followed the lessons. This list will repeat some of those already mentioned, just to make sure you have a fresh supply for a really good curry. I have put them in order of importance and not alphabetically.

Herbs and Spices
*Chilli powder or cayenne
    pepper*
Coriander, ground
Cumin
Turmeric
Cardamoms
Cinnamon
Clove powder
Curry leaves
Methi (fenugreek leaves)
Ginger, fresh or dried
Mustard seeds

Tamarind
Bay leaves
Other ingredients
Chapati flour
Gram flour (chick pea flour)
Brown rice flour
Soya flour
*Ghee (clarified butter — not
    essential as you can use oil)*
*Sesame seed oil (safflower oil is a
    good substitute)*
Surinam brown rice
Lentils or split peas

One of the most popular sessions in my cookery course is Indian cookery. The students seem to love the food. For many of them it is the first time that they have tasted a curry without the commercial curry powder mix in it. Unfortunately, most Indian restaurants do not cook real Indian food at all. One curry invariably tastes just like another. This is a great pity because the right combination of spices together with the right choice of meat or vegetables presents the food at its tastiest best. Another point is that in the making of chapatis, puris and samosas (see page 104 for recipes), I use wholemeal chapati flour, *ata*, which is what the Indians used traditionally in their baking until the Western mania for refined food hit them. It is a very finely milled wholemeal flour which is lighter than the variety of wholemeal flour we generally use in the West. I also use Surinam brown rice (see notes on grains page 44) which is the nearest to refined white Basmati rice, so popular with curries, that I have found.

In the lesson it is only possible to reveal a few of the delightful secrets of the Indian kitchen but I trust that my choice will add to whatever knowledge you already have of this wonderful cuisine, and help your recipes to be authentic in taste and a joy to your palate. Forget the packets of curry powder and learn to create a variety of flavours by mixing your own spices to suit different dishes. Both curry powder and garam masala are mixtures of spices which you do not need to buy once you become familiar with the individual spices I have listed. My spice list, with hints on making your own curry powder mixture, is only touching the surface of this style of cooking but it is a step in the right direction.

Essential Spices

The list is not in alphabetical order, but arranged in such a way that you can add to your store as you become more adventurous.

CHILLI POWDER or CAYENNE PEPPER. Both of these spices make the dish hot and give it a reddish colour. Use too much and you end up with lots of heat and no subtle flavour from the other ingredients used. Cayenne is a superior chilli powder. To achieve a red colour use *PAPRIKA PEPPER* (packed with vitamin C). Although part of the chilli family it is mild in flavour and not hot.

CORIANDER SEEDS AND LEAVES. This spice gives a beautiful flavour when used simply on its own with, for example, sautéd red cabbage or courgettes. The powder obtained by grinding the seeds is an essential ingredient in curry powder mixtures. The leaves, which look like French parsley, can be used in much the same way as parsley but will provide a different flavour. Great chopped up in salads.

CUMIN. From the same family as coriander, this spice is slightly stronger in flavour — again a principal ingredient in curries.

TURMERIC. Care must be taken not to use too much of this spice. It has a very strong, pungent flavour and is a vital ingredient in the making of curry dishes. The yellow pigment is often used to dye materials and when saffron is too expensive or unobtainable, you can use turmeric to colour your rice yellow. Just 1 teaspoon (5ml) added to the rice and water before cooking will do the trick.

CARDAMOM. Comes in either green or white pods. The green pods are stronger in flavour. You need so few of these marvellous seeds and, although they are quite expensive, a little goes a long way to perfect your curries or sweet dishes. They can be used whole, or the pods cracked and the tiny seeds inside crushed and added to the dish. After a meal, a pod may be chewed to sweeten the breath, or as a digestive.

CINNAMON POWDER or STICKS. I use the powdered cinnamon in sweet dishes and the sticks in curries and Dhal (see page 102). Chewing cinnamon sticks is said to strengthen the gums as well as sweeten the breath.

CLOVES. Oil of cloves is an antiseptic. I mostly use powdered cloves in minute proportions when making curry powder mixture and in cake baking.

CURRY LEAVES. Taste and smell like a good curry mixture all on their

Opposite Mixed Vegetable Curry (see page 100).

own. You can buy them fresh from Indian emporiums. Dry them and store in an airtight container.

FENUGREEK LEAVES AND SEEDS (METHI). Again, like curry leaves, fenugreek leaves have a distinctive curry smell and flavour of their own. In my curries I use one or the other of these leaves. The seeds are great sprouted and then stirred into sauces, or just lightly toasted before adding to your dishes.

GINGER, DRIED or FRESH. I prefer to use grated fresh ginger whenever possible. It is milder in flavour than the dried. A 1in (2·5cm) knob of fresh ginger grated into any curry sauce makes all the difference. I also use it in cakes with a little powdered ginger to give a stronger flavour of ginger and in Sweet and Sour Sauce (see page 125).

MUSTARD SEEDS. Black or white, these seeds are a good addition to your curries but must be used sparingly. White seeds are the black ones with the outer skin rubbed off. Black mustard seeds are usually preferred in Indian cooking as they have a stronger flavour.

TAMARIND. The fruit of the tamarind tree is very tart with a citrus-like taste. You can substitute the juice of a small lemon for this ingredient, but nothing quite takes the place, for flavour, of tamarind. All you do is soak the dried fruit, which has very hard, stone-like seeds in it, in warm water for 1 hour. Then squash all the mixture through a sieve. You will have a tangy, thickish liquid which you just stir into your curry. Well worth trying to obtain.

Other Basic Ingredients

CHAPATI FLOUR (ATA). A type of wholemeal flour which takes on a slightly stickier consistency when made into dough. It makes much lighter Indian-type unyeasted breads and Samosas (see page 104 for recipes) than if you use ordinary wholemeal flour.

GRAM FLOUR (BESAN). This is ground chick peas. Marvellous for Pakora (see page 105), which is a selection of vegetables dipped in batter and deep fried. Other bean flours are used in Indian cooking such as mung bean and pea flours. Full of protein, they have many variable uses.

BROWN RICE FLOUR (white is usually sold but try and get brown). I use this in pancakes and in Pakora batter. It adds goodness and crispness. Great added to soups as a thickener. It also makes a lovely white sauce instead of using wheat flour.

GHEE. Often an ingredient in Indian recipes, this is clarified butter or margarine. To make it you just heat the butter or margarine in a thick saucepan and simmer for 1 hour. Strain it and store in a jar. I must say I prefer to use a good oil such as sunflower or safflower oil instead of ghee.

SESAME SEED OIL. Absolutely lovely but very expensive. In some parts of India this and mustard oil (a very strong oil) are often used instead of ghee. I only use sesame seed oil for special salads or stir-fry dishes where you truly taste its delicious flavour.

Opposite *(top right)* Dhal (see page 102, *(bottom left)* Puris (see page 104).

Curry Spice Mixture

Before I begin the recipes, here is a good standby curry spice mixture. This makes enough for four good size mixed vegetable or meat and vegetable curries (use less if you wish, it could do for six to eight milder curries).

2 level tablespoons (30ml) turmeric
2 level tablespoons (30ml) cumin
2 level tablespoons (30ml) coriander
just under 1 level tablespoon (15ml) chilli powder or cayenne pepper (less if you wish)

16 cardamoms, podded
1 level teaspoon (5ml) clove powder
1 level tablespoon (15ml) black mustard seeds, crushed

Mix all the spices together and place in an airtight container.

When you come to make your curry you can add a cinnamon stick, fresh ginger, methi (fenugreek leaf) or curry leaves, and tamarind if you wish. For one good size curry you will need 2 level tablespoons (30ml) of your jarred mixture, adding the other ingredients mentioned if you wish.

Mixed Vegetable Curry *(illustrated on page 98)*

This curry is a great success with all who sample it. Refer to the list in the introduction for information on any ingredient not familiar to you. The spices are authentic but the vegetables are my own popular mix up. Big thick pot essential!

Serves 6.

1 level dessertspoon (10ml) turmeric
1 level dessertspoon (10ml) cumin
1 level dessertspoon (10ml) coriander
1 dessertspoon (10ml) methi
1 level teaspoon (5ml) cayenne pepper or chilli powder
4 cardamoms podded and seeds ground
2 cinnamon sticks
¼ teaspoon clove powder
1in (2·5cm) knob fresh ginger, grated
1 level teaspoon (5ml) black mustard seeds
4 tablespoons (60ml) sunflower oil for frying
2 medium onions, peeled and chopped
3 cloves garlic, crushed
2 medium carrots, scrubbed and cut into 1in (2·5cm) sticks
2 medium potatoes, scrubbed, steamed for 10 minutes and chopped in ¾in (2cm) cubes — leave skins on

3 celery sticks, chopped
½ medium cauliflower, cut into florets
1 green pepper (or ½ red, ½ green), de-seeded and chopped
1 small cooking apple, chopped (leave skin on)
1 tablespoon (15ml) wholemeal flour, to thicken mixture slightly (optional)
6 fresh tomatoes, skinned and chopped or 14oz (396g) can tomatoes
1 tablespoon (15ml) tomato purée
6oz (175g) French beans, frozen or fresh (leave whole)
½ pint (275ml) water
2oz (50g) tamarind (soaked, then sieved) or juice of 1 lemon and a curl of lemon rind
sea salt to taste (a stock cube is very good to use in this recipe instead of the salt)

Get the spices ready on a plate before you start.

Heat the oil in large, thick saucepan. Sauté the onion, garlic and carrots for 7 minutes, add the potatoes and celery and sauté for another 5 minutes. Add the cauliflower, peppers and apples and continue frying for

3 minutes only. Stir in all the spices and fry for just 2 minutes. Take care not to burn the mixture. Add the flour and stir well in. Finally add the tomatoes, tomato purée, beans, water, tamarind or lemon juice and rind and sea salt or stock cube to taste. Do not mush the mixture. Just gently stir the juices with the spices and vegetables then bring to the boil over medium heat. Turn down to simmer and cook for 45 minutes with the lid on tightly.

Serve with Surinam long grain rice (see page 44). For a choice of side dishes including Hot Lime and Peach Chutney (see page 126) and Yoghurt Bowl Cooler (page 130).

Green Vegetable Curry

Very mild and subtle in flavour.

Serves 4.

1 heaped teaspoon (10ml) coriander
1 heaped teaspoon (10ml) cumin
1 heaped teaspoon (10ml) turmeric
½ teaspoon black mustard seeds
¾ teaspoon chilli powder or cayenne pepper
1 heaped teaspoon (10ml) fresh ginger root, grated
3 cardamoms, podded
2 bay leaves or 1 level dessertspoon (10ml) curry leaves
juice of 1 small lemon and a curl of lemon rind
2 medium onions, peeled and chopped

2 large cloves garlic, crushed
4 tablespoons (60ml) safflower or sunflower oil or ghee
2 medium potatoes, scrubbed, diced with skins on and boiled for 10 minutes in salted water
1 small green pepper, de-seeded and chopped
1 medium cauliflower, cut in florets
1 heaped tablespoon (30ml) fresh coconut, grated or desiccated
½ pint (275ml) water (use that which potatoes were boiled in)
sea salt to taste

Mix all the spices with the lemon juice and rind. Fry the onion and garlic in the oil or ghee for 5 minutes. Add the potatoes and continue frying for another 3 minutes. Add the lemon and spice mixture and fry for 2 minutes (take care not to let the mixture burn). Stir in the green pepper and cauliflower and stir over a low heat for 1 minute. Finally add the coconut, water and sea salt to taste. Put the lid on and cook on a low heat for 25 minutes or until the cauliflower is cooked but not mushy.

I serve this with dhal and chapatis.

French Bean or Okra Curry with Mushrooms

Serves 4.

This is a variation of the Green Vegetable Curry. Simply omit the cauliflower from the previous recipe and add either 1lb (450g) French beans, fresh or frozen, or 1lb (450g) okra, plus 6oz (150g) sliced button mushrooms. It tastes quite different and adds yet another curry to your repertoire.

Dhal *(illustrated on page 99)*

For this recipe you can use red split lentils, continental green lentils, green or yellow split peas or tiny brown lentils. Soak them for 1 hour at least.

8oz (225g) lentils or **split peas, soaked for 1 hour**
sea salt
1 large onion, peeled and chopped
2 tablespoons (30ml) oil
1 fresh chilli, chopped or **½ teaspoon cayenne pepper (optional)**
1 level teaspoon (5ml) mustard seeds

6 black peppercorns, crushed
1 teaspoon (5ml) cumin seeds, crushed
1 teaspoon (5ml) coriander seeds, crushed
1 teaspoon (5ml) turmeric
1 teaspoon (5ml) fresh ginger root, grated
2 tablespoons (30ml) lemon juice or **lime juice (even better)**

Drain the lentils or peas, add 3 cups (about 1 pint (550ml)) of fresh, cold water and a little sea salt, bring to the boil and simmer gently with the lid on for about 30 minutes, until the water is absorbed and the mixture is thick and mushy. Sauté the onion in the oil for 10 minutes until lightly browned. Add all the spices except the ginger and lemon or lime juice and stir into the onion for 2 minutes over a low heat. Take off the heat, stir in the ginger and lemon or lime juice and mix with the cooked lentils.

This is a marvellous protein booster to serve with vegetable curries or with chapatis and yoghurt for a wholesome meal that is simple and delicious.

Spicy Courgettes with Pine Kernels

Serves 4.

1 large onion, peeled and sliced
2 cloves garlic, crushed
4 tablespoons (60ml) ghee or **sunflower oil**
2 sticks celery, chopped
½ red and ½ green pepper, de-seeded and chopped
4 medium courgettes, washed and sliced
2oz (50g) tamarind, soaked and sieved (see page 99)
1 teaspoon (5ml) coriander
1 teaspoon (5ml) cumin
1 teaspoon (5ml) turmeric
¼ teaspoon clove powder
1 cinnamon stick

3 cardamoms, podded and seeds crushed
1 heaped teaspoon (10ml) methi (fenugreek leaf)
1 knob fresh ginger, grated (about 1 heaped teaspoon (10ml))
1 fresh chilli, finely chopped or **½ teaspoon chilli powder** or **cayenne pepper**
6 tomatoes, skinned and chopped
1 tablespoon (15ml) tomato purée
6 tablespoons (90ml) water
2oz (50g) pine kernels
fresh coriander or **parsley leaves to garnish**

Sauté the onion and garlic in the oil for 5 minutes. Add celery, green and red pepper and sauté for 3 minutes then add the courgettes and continue to fry for 3 minutes more. Add all the spices and stir on a low heat for 2 minutes. Finally add the tomatoes, tomato purée and water. Stir in well. Put the lid on and cook for 25 minutes on a low heat. Toast the pine kernels in a dry pan for a few minutes.

Serve surrounded by brown Surinam rice (see page 44). Sprinkle the pine kernels on top and garnish with coriander or parsley leaves.

Right Samosas (see page 105).

Below Pakora (see page 105).

The following three recipes help to complete a true Indian meal. All made from the one basic unyeasted dough.

Basic Unyeasted Dough

12oz (350g) wholemeal chapati flour (ata) **good pinch salt**	**3 tablespoons (45ml) safflower** or **sunflower oil** or **ghee** **8fl oz (250ml) water**

Sift the flour and salt and rub in the oil (slightly warmed) or melted ghee. Gradually add the water to make a smooth dough then knead for 10 minutes. Cover with a damp cloth or place in a greased plastic bag and leave to rest for 1 hour.

Chapatis

Using the basic unyeasted dough you can make approximately 10-12 chapatis.

Divide the dough into balls. Take one ball between the palms of your hands, flatten it and flip it from palm to palm a few times, then roll it out on a well-floured board to approximately 7in (18cm) in diameter. Roll out one at a time, keeping the remaining dough covered or it will dry out.

Heat a thick frying pan or griddle. When it is very hot, pop in the chapati and press it gently with a large spoon to encourage it to bubble in places. When the bottom of the chapati is turning brown flip it over and cook the other side. These can be eaten with a curry instead of rice.

Puris *(Illustrated on page 98)*

Have hot oil ready as for deep frying. The basic unyeasted dough makes 24 puris.

Pinch off walnut sized pieces of dough, form into balls, and flatten each with an oiled rolling pin on an oiled board to about 3in (8cm) in diameter. Heat oil for deep frying and drop the puris in one at a time. As the puri pops up to the surface press it gently with the back of a spoon. It will puff up like a balloon. When golden, turn over and cook the other side. Great fun and deliciously light in texture.

Samosas (Stuffed pasties) *(Illustrated on page 103)*

You will need oil for deep frying. The basic unyeasted dough makes 16 samosas.

Filling
1 medium onion, peeled and finely chopped
3 tablespoons (45ml) sunflower oil or **ghee**
1 tablespoon (15ml) fresh ginger, grated or **1 level teaspoon (5ml) dried ginger**
1 teaspoon (5ml) coriander
1 teaspoon (5ml) cumin

1 teaspoon (5ml) turmeric
1 level teaspoon (5ml) cayenne pepper or **chilli powder**
1 tablespoon (15ml) lemon juice
2 large potatoes, scrubbed, diced in ½in (1cm) cubes and steamed until cooked
1 teacup frozen peas (pop in boiling water then drain)
oil for deep frying

Sauté the onion in the oil or ghee for 5 minutes. Add the spices and lemon juice and cook on a low heat for 2 minutes. Add the potatoes and peas and stir gently, coating the vegetables with the spices, and continue to cook for another 2 minutes. Let the mixture get cold. Cover it to keep the aroma and flavour sealed in.

Take one quarter of the dough and roll it out on a lightly floured board. Fold it in half and roll out again. Repeat, then roll it out for a third time to approximately 18in (46cm) square. Cut into four. Place 1 tablespoon (15ml) of the cooled filling on each small square. Form into an envelope shape by putting two opposite corners of the dough into the centre then fold the other two corners over this. Dampening the edges with a little beaten egg and water helps enormously. Deep fry in hot oil and see them disappear as soon as you make them!

Pakora (Deep fried vegetables in batter) *(Illustrated on page 103)*

Try this recipe and get hooked on a real healthy munchie!

Batter
4oz (110g) gram flour (chick pea flour)
2oz (50g) soya flour
2oz (50g) brown rice flour
1 level teaspoon (5ml) cayenne pepper (optional)

1 level teaspoon (5ml) coriander (optional)
1 level teaspoon (5ml) sea salt
1 level teaspoon (5ml) baking powder
12fl oz (350ml) cold water

Sieve the flours into the mixing bowl with the spices, salt and baking powder. Gradually add the water to form a smooth, creamy batter. Best if left to stand, covered, for 1 hour.

The vegetables are a matter of choice. My favourites are onion rings, cauliflower florets, whole button mushrooms, sliced courgettes, sliced aubergines and slices of potato. Sprigs of parsley are also delicious. Dip the vegetables individually into the batter and deep fry in hot oil until golden. A small plate of diced or sliced vegetables will make a large plate of pakora. I sprinkle shoyu over these just before serving. These are always a winner.

Sprouting Seeds, Salads and Dressings

LESSON 9

SHOPPING LIST

I will not list fresh vegetables as these vary from season to season. For good dressings, cold pressed oils are, I think, essential.

Sprouting seeds. *(You can buy special mixed packs of these seeds but I think it is best to buy a variety of seeds and sprout them individually)*
Alfalfa seed, for sprouting
Aduki beans, for sprouting
Mung beans, for sprouting
Whole lentils, for sprouting
Whole wheat, for sprouting
Triticale, for sprouting (very difficult to obtain)

Olive oil (virgin olive oil is best)
Safflower oil (cold pressed)
Sunflower oil (cold pressed)
Sesame seed oil (cold pressed)
Clear honey
Cider vinegar
Mustard powder
Fresh garlic
Grated horseradish (in a jar)

Fresh, raw vegetables and fruit are one of the best aids to health we can treat ourselves to. Salads can be boring or extremely exciting. In this lesson I will try to enhance these health-giving foods with flavour that will encourage you to prepare and enjoy at least one good salad each day. Included in the lesson are salads of which there are hundreds of variations and a variety of dressings, some of which will be familiar to you while others are possibly less well known.

In making my dressings I always use cold pressed oils. See the introduction (page 9) where I have discussed the importance of these oils. Cider vinegar is also my preference where vinegar is an ingredient in recipes. It is reputed to help maintain the balance between the acids and alkalis in the body and contains a wealth of minerals.

Sprouted Seeds

Another highly nutritious must I cannot praise enough are bean sprouts. You can purchase Chinese bean sprouts very inexpensively in supermarkets and from greengrocers. These are sprouted from the mung bean but you can sprout many beans and grains at home with great success. The nutritional value varies according to the variety of seed you sprout but generally they are all rich in vitamins B and C and have a high level of protein. Sprouted vegetables are higher in vitamin C and grains are a richer source of vitamin B. Very small traces of vitamin B_{12}, the vitamin supposed to be missing in a plant diet, are sometimes found in sprouted seeds. I will list just a few which I think are good to start off with but there are many more to choose from once you begin sprouting your own.

Bean Sprout Salad with
Mushrooms, Chinese style (see
page 109).

ALFALFA SEEDS sprouted contain 40 per cent protein and are a rich
source of vitamins and minerals. The sprouts are thin and light in texture
like mustard cress but the flavour is quite different.

ADUKI BEANS sprouted contain 25 per cent protein, several amino
acids and a good supply of vitamins B and C.

MUNG BEANS sprouted contain 37 per cent protein and are very rich in
the B complex vitamins and vitamin C. Commercially sold bean sprouts
are usually mung beans.

LENTILS sprouted contain 25 per cent protein, are nutty in flavour and
again a good source of vitamins B and C. Do not use split lentils. The
whole small brown lentils or continental green lentils sprout well.

WHOLE WHEAT sprouted contains a good supply of minerals and the B complex vitamins. The right time to eat these sprouts is when they are ½in (1cm) long, no bigger. Great to add to your bread recipes (see page 14 for Bread with a Different Flavour).

TRITICALE sprouted. These seeds are a cross between rye and wheat and not too easy to come by. They are 30 per cent protein and contain 19 amino acids, a good supply of vitamins B, C, D, E and F and lots of fibre.

Sprouting your own seeds

You can buy seed sprouters which take the guesswork out of the whole operation and make sure that the seeds do not sit in stagnant water. They are usually in three tiers so you can have three lots of seeds going at the same time in the one container. You can, however, successfully sprout seeds in a glass jar.

Wash the seeds well and pick them over for stones, etc. Leave to soak in water for 2 hours then drain. Place the seeds in the jar. Put a piece of muslin over the opening and secure it with an elastic band. Rinse the seeds three times daily with warm water and let the water drain out through the muslin cloth by placing the jar on its side. They do not need to be in the dark but must be drained well after each rinsing. Soaking for 2 hours before placing them into the sprouting jar will speed the whole process up. Keep the jar in a warm place but not in direct sunlight — a room temperature of 60/65°F (18°C) is about right. The time the seeds take to sprout varies but usually it is 3-6 days at the most.

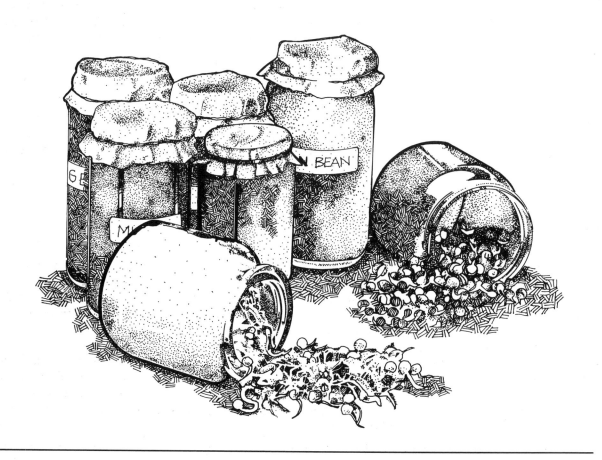

Mediterranean Salad

Here is a fantastic salad to start the lesson. Only for special occasions. Make a huge bowlful, you will need it!

2 medium potatoes, steamed, peeled and cubed
1 small green pepper, de-seeded and chopped
1 small red pepper, de-seeded and chopped
6oz (175g) piece bulb fennel, sliced
2 medium courgettes, washed, chopped into 1in (2·5cm) sticks, soaked in cider vinegar for 10 minutes, then drained

1 small onion, peeled and finely chopped
4 large tomatoes, chopped into segments
1 teaspoon (5ml) oregano
2 tablespoons (30ml) fresh parsley, chopped
crisp lettuce leaves (cos or Webb) to serve
3 large eggs, hard-boiled and 12 olives, halved, for garnish

Mix all the ingredients except the lettuce, eggs and olives. When ready to serve, scoop large spoonfuls of the salad on to the crisp lettuce leaves. Top with the olives and sliced egg. Pour Olive Oil and Lemon Dressing (see page 115 for recipe) generously over this.

Bean Sprout Salad with Mushrooms (Chinese style) *(illustrated on page 107)*

10oz (275g) bean sprouts
4oz (110g) button mushrooms, washed and sliced
1 small green pepper, de-seeded and finely chopped
1 carrot, scrubbed and very thinly sliced

1 small bunch spring onions, chopped (leave green stems on)
2 tablespoons (30ml) pineapple, fresh or canned, chopped (optional)

Mix all the ingredients together and pour about ½ teacup of Sweet and Sour Dressing (see page 114 for recipe), over this, coating the vegetables well. It is a good idea to dress this salad 30 minutes before serving to let the flavours merge.

Chinese Leaf Salad with Toasted Pumpkin Seeds *(Illustrated on page 110)*

Chinese leaves are a cross between white cabbage and lettuce and very economical. They will last up to 2 weeks in the fridge in a plastic bag if they are fresh when bought. Cut lengthwise there will be enough to make two large bowls of salad from one good sized head.

1 large green eating apple cut in small chunks (leave skin on)
½ good sized head Chinese leaves
1 punnet mustard cress or 1 bunch watercress, chopped

½ small onion, peeled and very finely chopped
2oz (50g) pumpkin seeds toasted in a dry pan for a few minutes

Put the apple in a bowl of lemon juice and water to prevent it going brown while you prepare the salad. Shred the Chinese leaves as thinly as possible and mix all the ingredients together. Sprinkle the toasted seeds on top. Pour cold pressed Sunflower or Safflower Dressing (see page 115) over this just before serving.

Red or White Cabbage Salad with Pecan Nuts *(illustrated above)*

Red cabbage is slightly stronger in taste than the white variety and makes a nice change.

1½lb (700g) red or white cabbage
2 green eating apples, chopped
   (leave skins on)
a little lemon juice
2oz (50g) raisins or sultanas
1 small onion, peeled and very
   finely chopped

2 tablespoons (30ml) fresh
   parsley, chopped
2oz (50g) pecan nuts, roughly
   chopped

(top) Red Cabbage Salad with Pecan Nuts, *(bottom)* Chinese Leaf Salad with Toasted Pumpkin Seeds (see page 109).

Shred the cabbage as finely as possible. Using a machine for this is best, but with a sharp knife it will shred thinly enough. Soak the apples in a little lemon juice and water while you prepare the salad. Mix all the ingredients together and pour over ¾ teacup of Horseradish Dressing (see page 114) 10 minutes before serving.

French Bean Salad with Toasted Sesame Seeds *(illustrated below)*

1lb (450g) French beans, frozen or
  fresh
1 tablespoon (15ml) sesame seeds
3 tablespoons (45ml) olive oil
**1 tablespoon (15ml) fresh lemon
  juice**

**1 large clove garlic, crushed
sea salt and freshly ground black
  pepper**

(left) Potato Salad with Chutney (see page 112), *(right)* French Bean Salad with Toasted Sesame Seeds.

If fresh, top and tail the beans, immerse in boiling, salted water and cook for 5 minutes until cooked but still crisp. If frozen, cook for 2 minutes only. Drain well. Toast the sesame seeds in a thick, dry pan over moderate heat for 5 minutes. Stir all the time and take care not to burn them. Add the olive oil, lemon juice and crushed garlic and stir over moderate heat for a further ½ minute only. Add salt and freshly ground black pepper to taste. Put the drained beans in a salad bowl and stir in the sesame seed mixture — beautiful!

Beetroot and Mint Salad

1½lb (700g) raw beetroot, grated
8oz (225g) firm salad tomatoes, cut
  into wedges
½ large cucumber, cut into sticks
  1in (2·5cm) long, soaked in cider
  vinegar for 30 minutes, then
  drained

1 tablespoon (15ml) fresh mint,
  finely chopped
1 teaspoon (5ml) mint, finely
  chopped, to garnish

Mix all the vegetables together with a fork. Add the tablespoon of mint carefully to avoid squashing the tomatoes too much. Stir in 1 cup Yoghurt Cheese or Sour Cream Dressing (see page 114) and garnish with the remaining mint.

Potato Salad with Chutney *(illustrated on page 111)*

2lb (1kg) potatoes, steamed, peeled
  and diced
4 sticks celery, finely chopped (use
  the inside stalks for salad, outside
  for soups)
1 teacup frozen peas, cooked for 2
  minutes and drained
1 teacup frozen sweetcorn, cooked
  for 2 minutes and drained
1 small onion, peeled and finely
  chopped

3 tablespoons (45ml) Peach
  Chutney (see page 126 for
  recipe) or any sweetish chutney
4 tablespoons (60ml) mayonnaise
  (see page 115 for recipe)
3 tablespoons (45ml) fresh
  parsley, chopped (leave some
  for garnish)

Mix all the ingredients together, taking care not to break up the potatoes. Sprinkle a little parsley on top to serve.

Saffron Rice Salad with Toasted Almonds

Delicious hot or cold.

1 large onion, peeled and chopped
2 cloves garlic, crushed
2 tablespoons (30ml) cold pressed
  sunflower or safflower oil
8oz (225g) short grain Italian brown
  rice
1 pint (550ml) hot stock or boiling
  water plus vegetable stock cube

pinch saffron or 1 teaspoon (5ml)
  turmeric
8oz (225g) frozen green peas (if
  fresh, cook until soft)
2oz (50g) almonds
¾ teacup Shoyu Dressing (see
  page 114 for recipe)
few sprigs parsley to garnish

In a thick saucepan sauté the onion and garlic gently in the oil for 10 minutes. Add the washed and well drained rice. Stir with the onions for 4 minutes until the rice begins to colour slightly. Add the stock with the saffron or turmeric and bring to the boil. Cover and simmer for 30 minutes. Do not stir. When cooked, the rice should have absorbed all the liquid.

While the rice is cooking place the peas in boiling, salted water for 5 minutes then drain. Blanch the almonds by putting them in very hot water for 5 minutes, peel the skins off and split the almonds in half. Toast them in a dry, thick pan, stirring constantly for 5 minutes until lightly browned. When the rice is cooked pour on ¾ teacup of Shoyu Dressing, fork in most of the toasted almonds and the peas, transfer to a flat serving plate, sprinkle the remaining almonds on top and surround with sprigs of parsley.

Orange, Tomato and Onion Salad

This is very simple and quite delicious.

**6 medium oranges, peeled and
    thinly sliced
1 medium onion, peeled and very
    thinly sliced**

**6 medium tomatoes, thinly sliced
2 tablespoons (30ml) fresh
    parsley, chopped
sprigs of watercress to garnish**

Arrange the slices of orange, onion and tomato overlapping all round a shallow serving dish. Sprinkle on the parsley and garnish with sprigs of watercress. Pour over about ½ teacup of Olive Oil and Lemon or Sunflower Oil Dressing (see pages 115 for recipes).

Salad Dressings

A salad dressing can make any mixture of vegetables into a mouth-watering experience. Feeding my family tonight I did not have any exotic vegetables, just carrots, cress, cucumber and onion, but with a simple shoyu dressing it tasted great. So although my salad recipes may be wonderful creations of complementary vegetables, you can make a salad with any fresh vegetables topped with a super dressing. I always make three times the amount of dressing I have given in the recipes. This encourages me to make more salads because the dressing is waiting there in the fridge to be used.

Shoyu Dressing

6 tablespoons (90ml) sunflower, corn or **safflower oil**
1 tablespoon (15ml) cider vinegar
1 clove garlic, crushed
¼ teaspoon mustard powder or **made mustard**

½ teaspoon clear honey
¼ teaspoon fresh ground black pepper
1½ tablespoons (20ml) shoyu (naturally fermented soy sauce)

Mix all the ingredients in a screw top jar. This is better than just stirring with a spoon as the flavours merge well together after a good shaking.

Sweet and Sour Dressing (with fresh ginger)

6 tablespoons (90ml) sesame seed or safflower oil
1½ tablespoons (25ml) cider vinegar or **lemon juice**
1½ tablespoons (25ml) shoyu (naturally fermented soy sauce)

1 teaspoon (5ml) clear honey
¼ teaspoon dried mustard powder
good pinch five spice or **allspice**
1 heaped teaspoon (10ml) fresh ginger, grated
1 large clove garlic, crushed

Put all the ingredients into a screw top jar and shake well. Leave to stand for at least 1 hour before pouring over the salad. This helps the flavours to merge and mature together a little.

Yoghurt Cheese or Sour Cream Dressing

To make 4oz (110g) yoghurt cheese, put 16fl oz (450ml) of natural live yoghurt in a piece of muslin cloth and let it drip overnight (see page 130 on making yoghurt).

4oz (110g) yoghurt cheese or **sour cream**
1 large clove garlic, crushed
2 tablespoons (30ml) lemon juice

½ teaspoon clear honey
¼ teaspoon sea salt
¼ teaspoon fresh ground black pepper

Mix all the ingredients together with a balloon whisk. Do not liquidise or the mixture will become too runny and lose its creamy consistency.

Olive Oil and Lemon Dressing

3 tablespoons (45ml) virgin (cold
  pressed) olive oil
1 tablespoon (15ml) lemon juice
½ level teaspoon sea salt
¼ teaspoon freshly ground black
  pepper (or more to taste)

1 clove garlic, crushed (optional
  but great)
½ level teaspoon clear honey
¼ teaspoon mustard powder or
  made mustard

Shake the lot in a screw top jar.

Here are three variations of this basic dressing.

Olive Oil and Cider Vinegar Dressing

Omit the lemon juice and add the same quantity of cider vinegar.

Sunflower or Safflower Oil Dressing

Omit the olive oil and add the same amount of cold pressed sunflower or
safflower oil.

Horseradish Dressing

Add 2 heaped teaspoons (20ml) grated horseradish (you can buy this in a
jar). Only use commercial horseradish sauce if the plain grated
horseradish is not available.

Never Fail Home-Made Mayonnaise

*I use cold pressed oil for this but it
will be equally successful in texture
if you are using semi-refined
sunflower or corn oil (see notes on
oils, page 9).*

8fl oz (250ml) sunflower or
  safflower oil
1 large egg
½ teaspoon mustard powder
½ teaspoon black pepper

½ teaspoon sea salt
2 tablespoons (30ml) cider vinegar
  or half and half lemon juice
  and cider vinegar

Place the egg, mustard powder, pepper, salt, vinegar/lemon juice, and
2fl oz (50ml) of the oil in a liquidiser. Cover. Switch on the machine to
low and blend together. Uncap and slowly stream in the remaining oil,
still on low speed. If it should curdle, just scoop it out, put another egg in
the blender and gradually add the curdled mixture to it.

For a real Italian-flavoured mayonnaise, use olive oil in the recipe and
blend in 2 cloves of garlic. Delicious with any salad which has potatoes or
olives in it.

It's not just an apple a day we need to keep the doctor away! Maybe a
salad a day might help.

LESSON 10

Soups, Sauces, Chutneys, Dips and Yoghurt Making

SHOPPING LIST

As with the list for salads in the previous lesson, I have not included the fresh vegetables. These will change with the seasons and what is in season is usually best.

You will also probably have many of the herbs and spices used in this lesson. I will list only a few extra ones that might not be on your shelf.

Vegetable stock cubes (or your favourite stock cubes), for quick stock
Unbleached white flour
Rice flour (for gluten-free sauce)
Dried peaches
Desiccated coconut

Herbs and Spices
Aniseed or fennel seeds (similar flavour)

Caraway seeds
Celery seeds or celery salt
Dill
Lemon thyme or thyme
Mace blades or ground mace
Mixed herbs
Nutmeg

Soups

To make a really good soup that will feed the family several hearty meals you are going to need a huge, heavy cooking pot, and, to enjoy home-made soup at its best, make your own Garlic French Bread (see page 16 for recipe) and have the cheeseboard ready. These foods are so basic but as the soup simmers and the bread bakes you will see what a dancing soul the kitchen acquires as the aroma wafts its way into all the nooks and crannies.

I know all this soup-making and home baking takes time but I have included some simple soup recipes that will take you just 10 minutes more to prepare than opening a can. I will give you only a few combinations of the beautiful vegetables available (like salads, there are endless ways of making them). Remember that you can make a good broth from any assortment of vegetables and grains, with the addition of herbs and spices, and it will invariably taste good.

Beetroot and Red Cabbage Soup *(illustrated on page 118)*

This is based on a Russian recipe called Bortsch. Unusual, tasty and delicious served with yoghurt or sour cream.

Serves at least 12.

3 tablespoons (45ml) sunflower or safflower oil
2 medium onions, peeled and chopped
1½lb (700g) red cabbage, shredded
1 teaspoon (5ml) dried dill
¼ teaspoon caraway seeds (optional)
2 bay leaves
6 medium beetroots, thinly peeled and grated
1 teaspoon (5ml) Barbados sugar
3 tablespoons (45ml) lemon juice
3½ pints (2 litres) stock or vegetable or chicken stock cubes dissolved in hot water
sea salt and freshly ground black pepper
few drops cider vinegar (optional)
thick natural yoghurt or sour cream to serve
little fresh chopped parsley to garnish

Heat the oil in a large, thick cooking pot and sauté the onion and cabbage for 5 minutes. Add the dill, caraway seeds and bay leaves. Stir in the beetroot, sugar and lemon juice, merging the flavours well together. Finally add the stock. Stir all together and bring to the boil. Taste at this stage. Depending on how salty your stock is you might need a little more sea salt. Grind some black pepper in and a few drops of cider vinegar if you wish. Let it simmer with the lid on for 15 minutes. Serve with dollops of thick natural yoghurt (see recipe on page 130) or sour cream. One dessertspoon (10ml) of either dropped into the centre of each serving and topped with a little freshly chopped parsley looks spectacular.

Leek and Potato Soup

Serves at least 12.

3 large potatoes, scrubbed and coarsely chopped
2 tablespoons (30ml) cold pressed sunflower oil
4 sticks celery, chopped (tougher outer stalks are ideal)
4 large leeks, split, trimmed, washed and coarsely chopped (leave as much green on as possible)
1 heaped teaspoon (10ml) dried dill
4 tablespoons (60ml) parsley, chopped
3 tablespoons (45ml) lemon juice
3½ pints (2 litres) hot water
sea salt or vegetable stock cubes to taste
1 teaspoon (5ml) cayenne pepper (optional)
1 level teaspoon (5ml) freshly ground black pepper

Sauté the potatoes in the oil for 3 minutes. Add the celery and leeks and continue frying for 2 minutes. Stir in the dill, parsley and lemon juice, coating the vegetables well and add the hot water. Sprinkle over a little sea salt or add stock cubes to taste, the cayenne and black pepper. Stir over low heat for ½ minute, taste and add more sea salt if needed then lid tightly and simmer for 30 minutes. Liquidise, then reheat slowly.

For an extra protein booster, instead of sprinkling grated cheese over this soup, you could liquidise some tofu (soya cheese) with the soup.

Above *(left)* Beetroot and Red Cabbage Soup (see page 117), *(right)* Pumpkin Soup.

Right Spring Vegetable Soup.

Pumpkin Soup *(illustrated above)*

Serves 6.

2lb (1kg) pumpkin, diced
3 large cloves garlic, crushed
2 tablespoons (30ml) safflower oil
1 level teaspoon (5ml) aniseed or fennel seeds, crushed
2 tablespoons (30ml) fresh parsley, chopped

14oz (396g) can tomatoes or, **even better, 1lb (45g) fresh tomatoes, skinned and chopped**
1 pint (550ml) water
sea salt and freshly ground black pepper

Sauté the pumpkin and garlic in the oil for 3 minutes. Add the aniseed or fennel seeds and parsley and continue to fry for 1 minute. Add the tomatoes and stir well in. Finally add the water, sea salt and black pepper to taste. Bring to the boil and simmer with the lid on for 20 minutes. Liquidise when slightly cooled and re-heat before serving.

Spicy Lentil Soup

For this you can use any variety of lentil or split pea (see notes on lentils, page 73). Lightly spiced, this is a very nourishing and tasty soup, similar to dhal but much thinner.

Gives 8 good servings.

8oz (225g) (dry weight) lentils
1 large onion, peeled and chopped
2 cloves garlic, crushed
1 tablespoon (15ml) sunflower or safflower oil
1 rounded teaspoon (7ml) ground coriander
1 level teaspoon (5ml) cumin
1 level teaspoon (5ml) cayenne pepper

1 level teaspoon (5ml) black mustard seeds
curl of lemon rind
2 tablespoons (30ml) fresh parsley, chopped
2 bay leaves
1¾ pints (1 litre) hot water plus 2 vegetable or chicken stock cubes
2 tablespoons (30ml) lemon juice

Wash and soak the lentils for 1 hour. Drain, discarding the soaking water. Sauté the onions and garlic in the oil until soft and then add the coriander, cumin, cayenne pepper, mustard seeds, lemon rind, parsley and bay leaves. Continue to fry gently for 2 minutes. Add the drained lentils and stir into the spices for 1 minute. Add the hot water and stock cubes. Bring to the boil and simmer for 30-40 minutes. When cooked, stir in the lemon juice.

Spring Vegetable Soup *(illustrated opposite)*

Light and fresh in flavour.

Serves 6-8.

1½ pints (850ml) stock or vegetable or chicken stock cube, dissolved in hot water
6 small new potatoes, scrubbed and diced (leave skins on)
2 medium carrots, scrubbed and thinly sliced
1 small onion, peeled and finely chopped
4oz (110g) green peas, fresh or frozen
4oz (110g) young green beans, chopped into 1in (2·5cm) pieces

8oz (225g) sweetcorn, frozen
½ small red pepper, de-seeded and chopped
½ small green pepper, de-seeded and chopped
1 tablespoon (15ml) fresh parsley, chopped
½ teaspoon thyme or (better still) lemon thyme
1 teaspoon (5ml) lemon rind, grated
freshly ground black pepper

Put the stock in large cooking pot and bring to the boil. Add the potatoes, carrots, onion, peas (if fresh) and beans. Lid and simmer for 10-15 minutes. Add the sweetcorn and chopped peppers (if the peas are frozen add them also). Now add the parsley, thyme or lemon thyme, lemon rind and freshly ground black pepper and continue to simmer for another 10 minutes only.

Whole and Hearty Vegetable Soup

This soup is a complete meal in itself.

Serves 8.

6oz (175g) soya beans (dry weight)
4oz (110g) pot barley (see notes on grains, page 46)
3 tablespoons (45ml) sunflower or corn or safflower oil
2 large onions, peeled and chopped
2 large cloves garlic, chopped (optional)
2 large carrots, scrubbed and sliced
1 small turnip, thinly peeled and diced
2 potatoes, scrubbed and diced
2 sticks celery, chopped (outside stalks with some green leaves on if possible)
2 tablespoons (30ml) fresh parsley, chopped

1 teaspoon (5ml) mixed herbs or bouquet garni
2 bay leaves
1 teaspoon (5ml) celery seeds
4 tomatoes, peeled, chopped and mixed with 2 tablespoons (30ml) tomato purée
1 tablespoon (15ml) lemon juice
1 large cup green peas (frozen will do)
freshly ground black pepper
approx 3 tablespoons (45ml) shoyu (naturally fermented soy sauce), to taste

Wash and soak the beans overnight (24 hours is even better). Change the soaking water 3 times if possible. Cook the beans in fresh water for 3 hours. Liquidise half the cooked beans with a little of the cooking water to a smooth paste. Keep the beans and purée aside. Wash and soak the barley overnight. Drain, saving the soaking water.

Heat the oil in a large, thick cooking pot and sauté the onion, garlic and well-drained barley on a medium to low heat for 3 minutes. Add the carrots, turnips, potatoes and celery and fry gently, stirring all the time, for 1 minute. Stir in the parsley, mixed herbs, bay leaves and celery seeds. Let the flavours merge as you stir for about 1 minute. Now add the cooked soya beans, puréed beans, tomatoes and tomato purée, barley soaking water, lemon juice and enough cold water to make 3½ pints (2 litres) in all. Bring the broth to the boil, stir well and simmer with the lid on for 30 minutes. Now stir in the frozen peas, shoyu and black pepper. Simmer gently for 7 minutes more.

Sauces

How many times have you thought, 'I won't do that recipe because it entails making a sauce'? Well, I hope my recipes for simple sauces and more exotic sauces for special occasions will encourage you to think differently. Sauces can make a very simple meal into a delight to the taste buds. Once you get the knack of preparing a few basic sauces the variations with the addition of vegetables, spices and herbs are endless.

For thinner sauces, just add ¼ pint (150ml) more liquid to the basic recipe. You can use wholemeal plain flour instead of unbleached white. Soya flour or brown rice flour (it is not dark) may be used to make gluten-free sauces.

I will start with a stock pot recipe, the juice from which will enhance any sauce or gravy you may wish to make. It is not essential, but adds that extra flavour which you cannot get from stock cubes mixed with hot water. You can, of course, use one stock cube to each pint of hot water to achieve a simple stock that will be quite adequate for most recipes, but nothing takes the place of the traditional stock pot juice.

The Stock Pot

Over two days you will be surprised how much water you throw away after cooking vegetables. Don't! Keep it in a bowl in the fridge and add to it to make your stock pot.

3 tablespoons (45ml) sunflower or **corn oil**
2 good size onions, peeled and coarsely chopped
1 large potato, scrubbed and chopped
2 carrots, scrubbed and coarsely chopped
3 sticks celery, chopped (outside tough stalks)
1 large clove garlic, crushed
3½ pints (2 litres) water (including any vegetable juice you might have)

cleaned potato peelings if available
any odds and ends of vegetables, such as bits of peppers, squashy tomatoes, etc.
3 tablespoons (45ml) parsley, coarsely chopped
1 level teaspoon (5ml) mixed herbs
1 tablespoon (15ml) tomato purée (optional)
2 tablespoons (30ml) lemon juice
6 black peppercorns, crushed
3 tablespoons (45ml) shoyu (naturally fermented soy sauce)

In a large, thick saucepan, sauté the onion, potato, carrots, celery and garlic in the oil for 3 minutes. Add everything else except the shoyu. Stir and bring to the boil, turn down the heat and simmer gently with a tight lid on for at least 1 hour. Strain through a sieve, squashing as much juice from the vegetables as possible. Stir in the shoyu to your own taste. The amount given seems to be about right.

The stock will keep in the fridge for 3 days or can be frozen in an ice cube tray and melted over a low heat when needed. Well worth the bother.

Basic White Sauce (simple method)

Makes ½ pint (275ml).

1oz (25g) unbleached white flour
½ pint (275ml) milk (cows' or **soya)**
1oz (25g) polyunsaturated margarine or **butter**
sea salt and freshly ground black pepper

1 blade mace or **¼ teaspoon ground mace** or **nutmeg**
1 small bay leaf

Mix the flour to a smooth consistency with 3 tablespoons (45ml) of the milk. Bring the rest of the milk to the boil, take off the heat and stir 2 tablespoons (30ml) of the hot milk into the flour and milk mixture. Then pour this into the boiled milk, stirring constantly. Return to a low heat and whisk with a balloon whisk to prevent lumps forming. Add the margarine or butter, a little sea salt, black pepper and mace. Simmer for 3 minutes to ensure the flour is cooked.

Basic White Sauce (roux method)

This method entails a little extra bother but will give a better flavour to your sauces. A roux, which thickens your sauce, is made by heating equal quantities of flour and fat for 3 minutes before adding the liquid. The secret is not to hurry this heating process. Have it on a low heat and stir constantly to ensure an even distribution of the heat and to prevent the flour and fat from burning.

Ingredients as for Basic White Sauce (simple method)

Melt the margarine or butter in a thick saucepan on low heat and, when melted, stir in the flour. Gently cook this mixture for 3 minutes, stirring constantly. Take off the heat and add the milk gradually, still stirring, until smooth. Add salt, pepper, mace and bay leaf. Return to the heat and either whisk with a balloon whisk or stir with a wooden spoon until the sauce reaches the boil and thickens. Simmer over a very low heat for 3 minutes, stirring frequently.

VARIATIONS

Basic White Sauce with Brown Rice Flour or Soya Flour
Marvellous for those who need a gluten-free diet. Use the Basic White Sauce (simple method) but use rice or soya flour instead of unbleached white flour.

The following sauces are variations of the Basic White Sauce recipe. You can use either the simple or the roux method to prepare them unless otherwise directed.

Cheese Sauce
To make a thick sauce suitable for cauliflower cheese or to accompany any cooked vegetables add ½ teaspoon dried mustard powder creamed with a little water and 3-4oz (75-110g) grated Cheddar cheese, mature or farmhouse, to the Basic White Sauce recipe.

When the sauce is cooked, take off the heat and stir in the cheese and mustard cream. Do not re-heat. Keep the sauce warm by standing the saucepan in hot water with a damp cloth over the top to avoid a skin forming.

Thinner Cheese Sauce suitable for Lasagne
To the Basic White Sauce add ¼ pint (150ml) more liquid, either milk or stock. (See page 89 for Lasagne recipe).

Onion Sauce
Boil 1 large peeled and chopped onion in slightly salted water for 15 minutes. Drain, saving the cooking liquid.

Make the Basic White Sauce, but use half milk and half the onion liquid. Omit the mace. When cooked, stir in the onion with ½ teaspoon allspice. Heat gently for 1 minute only. Add 1 tablespoon (15ml) finely chopped parsley. A little grated cheese is always a nice addition to onion sauce — stir it in when the sauce is cooked and off the heat.

Mushroom Sauce

Sauté 1 small onion, peeled and very finely chopped, with 4oz (110g) sliced button mushrooms in little oil for 3 minutes. Stir in 1 tablespoon (15ml) lemon juice and ½ teaspoon oregano. Stir this into the Basic White Sauce just before serving.

Lemon Sauce with Dill

For this sauce you will need to use ¼ pint (150ml) stock. To this add 1 level tablespoon (15ml) dried dill or 2 tablespoons (30ml) fresh dill. Simmer for 2 minutes and add this to ¼ pint (150ml) milk to make just over ½ pint (300ml) liquid in all.

Make a Basic White Sauce with this liquid but omit the bay leaf and mace. When the sauce is cooked add 2 tablespoons (30ml) lemon juice and 1 teaspoon (5ml) very finely grated lemon rind. Stir in gently and serve.

Great with any bean burgers, Millet and Cheese Croquettes (see page 51) or with fish. Best of all, poured over asparagus it is a real treat.

Brown Gravy Sauce

When not using meat juices as a basis for your gravy I'm afraid you will need the Stock Pot recipe (see page 121). There is no other way to real success. The roux method is also essential to achieve the best flavour. I use this for our Sunday Nut Roast (see page 93). This recipe will make just over 1 pint (550ml) of gravy.

3 tablespoons (45ml) sunflower oil
  or **polyunsaturated margarine**
1 large onion, peeled and
  chopped

3 rounded tablespoons (60ml)
  unbleached white flour or **half**
  unbleached white flour and half
  soya flour
1½ pints (850ml) stock

Heat the oil or margarine in a thick saucepan, add the chopped onion, cover and fry gently for 10 minutes until the onion is lightly golden in colour. Add the flour, stirring constantly until the mixture is a deep golden brown. Take off the heat and gradually stir in the stock. When the stock has blended with the onion and flour mixture, return to a low heat and cook, stirring all the time, until the sauce comes to the boil. At this stage it will thicken slightly. Keep on a low heat and simmer gently for 15 minutes. Strain and serve. Next time you will have to make double the quantity, meat stock or no meat stock, this gravy is so popular!

If a more savoury taste is required, just add a little shoyu. This will also darken the gravy slightly.

Italian Tomato Sauce

Makes 1¾ pints (1 litre).

4 tablespoons (60ml) olive oil
1 large onion, peeled and finely chopped
2 large cloves garlic, crushed
4 sticks celery, chopped (outside stalks)
1 small green pepper, de-seeded and chopped (optional)
2 bay leaves
2 tablespoons (30ml) fresh parsley, chopped
1 heaped teaspoon (10ml) basil

1 tablespoon (15ml) shoyu (naturally fermented soy sauce)
1 level teaspoon (5ml) clear honey
2 tablespoons (30ml) lemon juice
1 tablespoon (15ml) wholemeal flour, plain
1lb 12oz (794g) can tomatoes, chopped
2 tablespoons (30ml) tomato purée
little sea salt and freshly ground black pepper to taste

Sauté the onion and garlic in the olive oil for 5 minutes. Add the celery and green pepper and sauté for another 4 minutes with the lid on. Stir in the bay leaves, parsley, basil, shoyu, honey and lemon juice. Heat through, blending the ingredients well together. Stir in the flour, simmer gently for 1 minute, then add the tomatoes, tomato purée and black pepper. Mix well together. Finally add a little sea salt if needed after tasting the sauce. A little will be enough. Simmer for 45 minutes with the lid on and then take out the bay leaves. Liquidise or strain the sauce through a sieve and heat through over a low heat before serving.

VARIATIONS

Chilli Tomato Sauce (or Falafal Sauce)
Add 1 good heaped teaspoon (10ml) coriander, the same amount of cayenne pepper or chilli powder or 3 fresh chillis, finely chopped, to the Italian Tomato Sauce recipe. Liquidise the sauce but do not strain. Stir 4 tablespoons (60ml) thick yoghurt or sour cream into the sauce after it is cooked and serve hot or cold.

Hungarian Paprika Sauce
Add 2 tablespoons (30ml) paprika pepper to the Italian Tomato Sauce recipe with the herbs, shoyu and lemon juice. When the sauce is cooked and off the heat, stir in 4 tablespoons (60ml) natural yoghurt mixed with 1 tablespoon (15ml) thick double cream. (This makes a good substitute for sour cream.)

Barbecue Sauce

This sauce keeps very well for 10 days in the fridge or freezes in ice cube trays.

1 tablespoon (15ml) tomato purée
1 tablespoon (15ml) cider vinegar
1 dessertspoon (10ml) molasses
1 level teaspoon (5ml) cayenne pepper
1 rounded teaspoon (10ml) paprika pepper

1 level teaspoon (5ml) mustard powder
just under 1 pint (550ml) Italian Tomato Sauce

Mix the tomato purée, cider vinegar and molasses together. Add the cayenne pepper, paprika and mustard powder to make a smooth paste and stir this into the Tomato Sauce. Lovely with cooked chick peas, haricot beans, soya beans and any bean burger, or *any* burger for that matter.

Sweet and Sour Sauce with Almonds or Cashews

This sauce is delicious stirred into a simple dish of plain boiled brown rice to which you have added green peas. Or poured over Pakora (deep fried battered vegetables, see page 105 for the recipe). Also great added to any mixture of stir-fried vegetables, bean sprouts, courgettes, carrots, peppers, etc.

2oz (50g) almonds or **cashews, blanched and split**
2oz (50g) **dried peaches, soaked in apple juice overnight**
1 tablespoon (15ml) **onion, peeled and very finely chopped**
1 large **clove garlic, crushed**
2 tablespoons (30ml) **sesame seed** or **safflower** or **sunflower oil**
1 teaspoon (5ml) **fresh ginger, grated**
1 level teaspoon (5ml) **five spice** or **allspice**

2 tablespoons (30ml) **dark brown sugar**
2 tablespoons (30ml) **shoyu (naturally fermented soy sauce)**
2 tablespoons (30ml) **cider vinegar**
2 tablespoons (30ml) **tomato purée**
1 level tablespoon (15ml) **arrowroot**
6fl oz (175ml) **water (or more if a thinner sauce is required)**

Toast the nuts in a dry pan, stirring constantly for 5 minutes. Mince, liquidise or sieve the peaches with 6fl oz (175ml) of the soaking juice. Sauté the onion and garlic in the oil for 10 minutes over a low heat until transparent. Take care that the mixture does not burn. Add the ginger and five spices and stir well into the onion. Mix all the other ingredients except the nuts, but including the water, together in a bowl. Still on a low heat, stir this mixture into the onions and spices and bring to the boil. Simmer gently for 3 minutes, stirring constantly. Add the toasted nuts just before serving.

Curry Sauce

Great for quick curries, poured over boiled eggs or mixed into plain boiled rice to make a delicious savoury rice. You can add chick peas or any cooked beans to make a simple curry to serve with rice or buckwheat.

1 large **onion, peeled and chopped**
2 large **cloves garlic, crushed**
3 tablespoons (45ml) **sesame seed oil, safflower oil** or **ghee**
1 teaspoon (5ml) **coriander**
1 teaspoon (5ml) **cumin**
1 teaspoon (5ml) **turmeric**
1 level teaspoon (5ml) **cayenne pepper** or **chilli powder**
¼ **teaspoon clove powder**
1 **cinnamon stick**
1 heaped teaspoon (10ml) **methi (fenugreek leaf)** or **4 bay leaves**

1 heaped teaspoon (10ml) **fresh ginger, grated**
1 teaspoon (5ml) **honey (optional)**
approx 6fl oz (175ml) **water** or **stock**
sea salt to taste
1 small **cooking apple, peeled and grated**
1 tablespoon (15ml) **tomato purée**
2oz (50g) **tamarind, soaked and sieved (see page 99)** or **2 tablespoons (30ml) lemon juice and a curl of lemon rind**

Sauté the onion and garlic in the oil or ghee for 7 minutes until pale gold in colour. Add the spices and cook on a low heat, stirring all the time, for 2 minutes. Add all the other ingredients and mix in well, cover and simmer on a low heat for 30 minutes.

Chutneys

Here is my favourite chutney recipe coming up.

Peach Chutney *(illustrated on page 47)*

Makes seven 1lb (450g) jars.

1· 1lb (500g) dried peaches
¾ pint (425ml) cider vinegar
12oz (350g) demerara sugar
1 large green pepper, de-seeded and chopped
1 medium red pepper, de-seeded and chopped
3 large cooking apples, peeled and chopped
6oz (175g) raisins

1 tablespoon (15ml) cayenne pepper
2 tablespoons (30ml) fresh ginger, grated
1 dessertspoon (10ml) coriander
¼ teaspoon clove powder
1 tablespoon (15ml) white or black mustard seed
6 large cloves garlic, crushed

Wash and soak the peaches for 24 hours, drain and chop. Put the vinegar and sugar in a large, thick saucepan and add all the other ingredients. Heat through for 3 minutes. Stir well, bring to the boil and simmer for 35 minutes with a lid on. Jar in the usual way if the family will let you get as far as the preserving pots!

The flavour is at its best after two weeks.

VARIATION

Hot Lime and Peach Chutney
This is a variation of Peach Chutney — fantastic with curries.

You will need ²/₃ of a jar of the Peach Chutney. Cut 1 lime into 16 pieces and soak in 4 tablespoons (60ml) cider vinegar with 1 rounded teaspoon (10ml) turmeric and 2 fresh chillies, finely chopped. Leave overnight, then cook on a low heat for 20 minutes until the lime is soft. Now add the Peach Chutney and reheat, stirring well together. Put into a clean, dry jar and leave for at least 24 hours before using. It improves with keeping.

Green Tomato Chutney

Makes eight 1lb (450g) jars.

1 level tablespoon (15ml) sea salt
3lb (1· 5kg) green tomatoes, skinned and chopped
2 large onions, peeled and chopped
1 large red pepper, de-seeded and chopped
approx 1 pint (550ml) cider vinegar

1lb (450g) demerara sugar
2 large cooking apples, peeled, cored and chopped
½ teaspoon ground cloves
1 teaspoon (5ml) mustard seeds
2 fresh or 4 dried chillis, chopped
1 teaspoon (5ml) allspice

Sprinkle sea salt over the tomatoes, onions and chopped pepper and leave for 1 hour, then drain well in a colander. Put the vinegar and sugar into a thick saucepan, then add all the other ingredients. Bring to the boil and simmer gently with a lid on for 30-35 minutes, then jar.

Coconut Chutney

This simple chutney is not for preserving. It is often served with curries and made just before serving. Fresh coconut is best but dried will do.

4oz (110g) fresh or **dried coconut, grated**

1 dessertspoon (10ml) fresh ginger, grated

¾ teaspoon cayenne pepper or **2 fresh chillis (de-seeded and finely chopped)**

2 tablespoons (30ml) onion, peeled and very finely chopped

3 tablespoons (45ml) fresh lemon juice or **2 tablespoons (30ml) cider vinegar**

Liquidise the coconut to a powder and fork in the other ingredients thoroughly.

Carrot and Cucumber Chutney

Another fresh chutney to be made just before serving. Like coconut chutney, it is often served in India with curries.

8oz (225g) carrots, scrubbed and very thinly sliced

8oz (225g) cucumber, chopped in small cubes

1 very small onion, peeled, finely chopped and crushed

1 dessertspoon (10ml) fresh ginger, grated

1 teaspoon (5ml) ground coriander

½ teaspoon cayenne pepper

3 tablespoons (45ml) lemon juice

4 tablespoons (60ml) natural yoghurt

little sea salt to taste

Mix all the ingredients together and serve as a side dish with curry.

Dips

I hope the next few recipes will enliven that very important meal of the day — lunch — or add that extra bowl to delight the buffet table. They make a nice healthy change from cheese, which seems to be a staple gap filler midway through the day.

Hummous (Middle Eastern Chick Pea Dip) *(illustrated on page 15)*

1· 1lb (500g) chick peas, washed, soaked, rinsed and cooked (see page 65)
juice of 4 lemons
3 tablespoons (45ml) olive oil (a must)
4 large cloves garlic, crushed

4 tablespoons (60ml) tahini (sesame seed paste)
sea salt to taste
freshly ground black pepper
little fresh chopped parsley to garnish

Retain some of the chick pea cooking water to liquidise the chick peas — but not too much. You want to end up with a thick, scoopable consistency. Liquidise the chick peas with the lemon juice, oil and garlic, gradually adding a little cooking water as you go along. Put into a serving bowl, stir in the tahini and add a little sea salt to taste. Grind a little pepper over the top and sprinkle on the chopped parsley.

A wonderful bowlful to dunk those crackers in at parties. Also, with Pitta Bread (see page 13 for recipe), crisp lettuce and watercress, this is a most satisfying and great-tasting lunch.

Soya Bean Spread 1

This is a highly nutritious and tasty way to eat soya beans, which can be so bland. To cook soya beans first for this recipe would be far too time-consuming. It is best to reserve this recipe for leftover beans, which freeze very well.

12oz (350g) (cooked weight) soya beans (see page 77 for cooking instructions)
1½ tablespoons (20ml) sunflower or safflower oil
1 small onion, peeled and very finely chopped
2 inner sticks of celery (tender sticks), very finely chopped

1 clove garlic, crushed (optional)
1 heaped teaspoon (10ml) oregano
½ teaspoon cayenne pepper (optional)
freshly ground black pepper to taste
1 tablespoon (15ml) shoyu (naturally fermented soy sauce)
2 tablespoons (30ml) tomato purée

Grind the cooked beans in a hand or electric cheese grinder. Put through a mincer if you wish. Sauté the onion, celery and garlic in the oil for a few minutes (it is important that they be chopped very finely). Add the oregano, cayenne pepper and black pepper. Mix the shoyu with the tomato purée, stir into the vegetables and simmer for 1 minute. Add the ground soya beans. Cool and use as a spread on toast or in sandwiches with any salad vegetables. It can also be used as a dip for parties.

Soya Bean Spread 2

12oz (350g) (cooked weight) soya beans (see page 77 for cooking instructions)

2 tablespoons (30ml) sunflower or safflower oil

1 small bunch spring onions, very finely chopped

2 tablespoons (30ml) green pepper, de-seeded and finely chopped

2 tablespoons (30ml) lemon juice

2 tablespoons (30ml) fresh parsley, chopped

½ teaspoon dried tarragon (optional)

1 tablespoon (15ml) shoyu (naturally fermented soy sauce)

freshly ground black pepper

Grind the cooked beans as in the previous recipe and mix well with the remaining ingredients.

Any beans will make a pleasant dip or sandwich filler. When you find a particular bean dish where the vegetables and herbs have just the right combination to your taste you can make dips with these very same ingredients. For example, Red Chilli Beans in Goulash Sauce is very popular. To make a dip out of this recipe just grind the cooked beans, add a little chilli powder, paprika, garlic, chopped green pepper, tomato purée and some natural yoghurt. Sprinkle on some fresh parsley to garnish and you have another dip.

Yoghurt and Yoghurt Cheese Making

Recipes including yoghurt have become more numerous in recent years. At last its value is being appreciated. There has been much research into the curative properties of yoghurt, and it is now accepted as a health-giving food. The bacteria in yoghurt can manufacture the B vitamins in the intestine so those who are taking antibiotics, which are known to cause severe deficiencies in this vital vitamin, would be well advised to eat yoghurt regularly. Also the bacteria in yoghurt kill harmful bacteria in the large intestine because they turn milk sugar into lactic acid and the harmful bacteria cannot live in the lactic acid.

Making your own yoghurt is not very difficult and is much cheaper than commercial brands. You can buy various yoghurt making gadgets which can help enormously but they are e known to cause severe deficiencies in this vital vitamin, would be well advised to eat yoghurt regularly. Also the bacteria in yoghurt kill harmful bacteria in the large intestine also act as a thickener. You can buy a culture, which gives instructions on the label but 2 tablespoons (30ml) of fresh live natural yoghurt should start you off well enough. Make sure that the yoghurt is live and without stabilisers. Try to avoid commercial sweet yoghurts as these invariably contain added sugar, colouring and stabilisers. A little honey or apple juice concentrate, plus mashed or chopped fruit, added to live natural yoghurt is both delicious and nourishing.

Yoghurt

1½ pints (850ml) skimmed milk or **full cream milk**

2 tablespoons (30ml) fresh live yoghurt or **1 packet yoghurt culture**

2 tablespoons (30ml) skimmed milk powder (optional)

Bring the milk to the boil, then turn down to simmer on very low heat. Simmer with the lid off for 10 minutes. Cool to a temperature of approximately 110°F (43°C). The milk should be still very warm but not burn your finger when testing. Stir in the milk powder. When thoroughly mixed, whisk in the yoghurt or yoghurt culture. Place the bowl of yoghurt mixture in a large, wide saucepan which contains enough hot water to reach half way up the yoghurt container. Cover the bowl of yoghurt mixture. Top up the saucepan with hot water several times to keep the right temperature and leave to stand for approximately 4 hours. Alternatively, you can put the yoghurt container in a warm airing cupboard, covered and wrapped in a hot towel.

Yoghurt Cheese

Very simply, put some live yoghurt into a piece of muslin, tie it and let it drip into a pan overnight. You will end up with what looks like curd cheese. It can be used instead of curd cheese or sour cream in any recipe.

Yoghurt Bowl Cooler

In India recipes with yoghurt, chopped raw vegetables and spices are called raiti. They complement any hot, spicy meal.

½ pint (275ml) live natural yoghurt
8oz (225g) diced cucumber
1 level teaspoon (5ml) clear honey
1 tablespoon (15ml) fresh mint, chopped

sea salt and freshly ground black pepper
½ teaspoon paprika pepper and 1 teaspoon (5ml) chopped fresh mint to garnish

Mix all the ingredients together and sprinkle on the paprika and chopped mint. You can add other spices such as ginger, cayenne pepper or a little curry powder mix.

Entertaining withWholefoods

LESSON 11

Friendship and eating well are two of the joys of life. Doing both at the same time by giving a dinner party means a double pleasure.

I think the reason I enjoy feeding my family and friends so much and teaching others how to cook healthy and delicious food is because I was skinny and always hungry as a kid. I can remember my first banana at the age of five or six. I think it must have been from the first shipload of fruit to arrive in Ireland after the war. My mother took us to the market one day and bought a hand of bananas. I can still recall the smell as she peeled down the skin layers. That first bite was a pleasure never again to be repeated with a banana. She also peeled an orange and gave us each some segments. The smell of that too was unbelievable.

I was also one of those kids who could never understand anyone leaving school lunch uneaten. To me, lunch was the best thing about school. That's a long time ago now and over the years various experiences have taught me to appreciate the food that grows and how to make the best of it. The menus I have devised will, I think, not only delight the palate but also be a pleasure to the eye, and they are well-balanced nutritionally. The quantities given will be enough for four good servings. Enjoy them to the full with a wine of your choice. Emphasis on health has been thrown to the winds a bit in this lesson but on special occasions I do think that we can allow ourselves a few delightful indulgences.

Each menu serves four.

Menu 1

Green Pea Soup with Wholemeal Croutons

Festive Nut Roast with Red Wine Sauce
Traditional Baked Potatoes
Baked Lemon Carrots
Braised Brussels Sprouts
Cranberry Sauce

Melon and Ginger Ice-cream

Green Pea Soup with Croutons

1lb (450g) peas, fresh or frozen (weight of fresh peas after podding)
1½ pints (825ml) water plus 1 vegetable stock cube
sprig of mint
small bunch of spring onions or 1 small onion, finely chopped
1 tablespoon (15ml) cold pressed sunflower oil or butter

2 level tablespoons (30ml) 81% (wheatmeal) flour, plain
½ teaspoon honey
sea salt and freshly ground black pepper
1 tablespoon (15ml) thick natural yoghurt
1 tablespoon (15ml) double cream
sprigs of mint and croutons to serve

Cook the peas with half the stock and the sprig of mint. If using fresh peas cook for 20-25 minutes, if frozen 7 minutes. In another pan sauté the spring onions or onion in the oil or butter until soft but not browned. Add the flour and stir with a wooden spoon until the mixture bubbles slightly. Remove from the heat and gradually add the remaining stock, stirring constantly. Cook gently, still stirring, until the sauce thickens. Cook for 2 minutes. Liquidise the cooked peas with their cooking water to a smooth purée. Sieve if not perfectly smooth. Blend the sauce with the pea purée and heat through. Add salt and pepper to taste. Stir in the cream and yoghurt just before serving. Garnish with sprigs of mint and croutons.

Wholemeal Bread Croutons

See page 13 for the bread recipe.

Cut slices of bread allowing half a slice for each serving bowl. Spread with butter. Place the slices on top of each other and cut into ¾in (2 cm) squares. Place on a baking tray and bake at 275°F, 140°C, Gas Mark 1 for 25-35 minutes depending on how fresh the bread is.

To give a garlic flavour just crush 1 clove of garlic into the butter and spread this on the slices of bread.

Festive Nut Roast and Vegetables *(illustrated on page 134)*

You will need a roasting tray and a 6 x 12in (15 x 30cm) piece of aluminium foil to cap roast. (See page 93 for a less expensive nut roast.)

Set the oven to 375°F, 190°C, Gas Mark 5.

4oz (110g) pistachio nuts (weighed after shelling)
2oz (50g) pine kernels
2oz (50g) pumpkin seeds
4oz (110g) almonds or hazel-nuts
1 medium onion, peeled and finely chopped (approx 6oz (175g))
2 tablespoons (30ml) shoyu (naturally fermented soy sauce)
3 tablespoons (45ml) cold pressed sunflower oil

2 standard eggs
3 tablespoons (45ml) fresh parsley, chopped
few pumpkin seeds for top of roast
2 tablespoons (30ml) cold pressed sunflower oil for sprinkling over the roast and accompanying potatoes

Grind the nuts and seeds so that they look like medium to fine breadcrumbs. (Not too powdery.) Mix all ingredients together, moulding well with your hands. Grease the roasting tray. Form the nut mixture into a loaf shape, flatten the top and place on the tray. Pour a little oil over the top and sprinkle on a few pumpkin seeds. Cap the roast loosely so that the foil does not stick to the roast. Leave to one side. Now prepare the accompanying vegetables. Steam sufficient potatoes for 20 minutes with the skins on. Peel thinly (save the peel for stock), and cut into halves or quarters depending on how big your potatoes are. Place around the roast. Sprinkle a little oil and a pinch of sea salt over the potatoes. Bake for 45 minutes in the pre-heated oven. Uncap the roast 5 minutes before the end of the cooking time.

Steam 1½lb (750g) scraped whole carrots for 7 minutes only. Slice them into slanted rings ½in (1cm) thick and place in a small casserole dish. Add 1oz (25g) butter or sunflower oil, 1 tablespoon (15ml) shoyu (naturally fermented soy sauce), 2 tablespoons (30ml) water and 1 tablespoon (15ml) lemon juice. Toss the carrots in this mixture, cover and put in the oven on a shelf just under the roast. These will be cooked when your roast is ready. They take about 30 minutes. Take them out if they are cooked sooner than this and keep warm.

Start braising the sprouts just 20 minutes before you serve the meal. Trim them and make a very slight cross cut in the base. Wash them well and steam for 10 minutes. Heat 1 tablespoon (15ml) sunflower oil or butter in a pan. Sauté ½ medium onion, cut into thin rings, until soft. This will take about 5 minutes. Pour in a little boiling, slightly salted water and a good pinch of freshly ground black pepper, add the steamed sprouts and simmer for 5 minutes. Baste the sprouts as they cook.

To serve the carrots and sprouts, place the sprouts in the centre of a serving plate, garnish with the onion rings and flute the edge of the dish with overlapping rings of baked carrots. Save the cooking juices of both vegetables and add this to your wine sauce or gravy.

Red Wine Sauce

Makes 1¼ pints (750ml).

It is always best to make a soup, sauce or gravy with water in which you have cooked vegetables. If this is not available then you can use a vegetable stock cube in hot water.

1 large onion, peeled and finely chopped
2 tablespoons (30ml) sunflower oil or **butter**
1 rounded tablespoon (20ml) 81% wheatmeal flour, plain
juices from vegetables (in this case, sprouts and carrots)
1 pint (550ml) vegetable stock
6 tablespoons (90ml) red wine
1 tablespoon (15ml) shoyu (naturally fermented soy sauce)
freshly ground black pepper to taste

Sauté the onion in the oil or butter until lightly browned. Shake in the flour from a dredger and let the mixture bubble gently for 1 minute. Blend in the vegetable juices and the hot vegetable stock very slowly, stirring continuously. Cook for 2 minutes. Strain and add the red wine, shoyu and freshly ground black pepper to taste. Heat through before serving.

Festive Nut Roast

Cranberry Sauce

This sauce is absolutely delicious and can be served with many savoury dishes. You can buy 10oz (275g) packs of cranberries in large supermarkets. Use jarred morello cherries if cranberries are not available. If using cherries, drain off the syrup, measure off 2fl oz (50ml) of the juice and discard the rest. Use the syrup and only 3fl oz (90ml) of the apple juice concentrate.

10oz (275g) cranberries
10oz (275g) cooking apples, thinly peeled, cored and chopped (weighed after peeling)
5fl oz (150ml) apple juice concentrate

2fl oz (50ml) water
4 tablespoons (60ml) cherry brandy or syrup

Cook all the ingredients except the brandy together for 20 minutes. (If using jarred cherries cook for 15 minutes only.) Add the brandy and reheat for 30 seconds. Jar and keep in the fridge when cool. The sauce will keep for 6 weeks even when opened.

Melon and Ginger Ice-cream

I use an Ogen melon for this recipe, though honeydew melon will do. The Ogen is orange with fine green lines. It is smaller and more rounded than honeydew and will stand firmly if you want to serve the ice-cream from the shell. If using a honeydew then a small one is correct for this recipe. You will need a small ball scoop if you wish to decorate the ice-cream with fresh melon balls soaked in the sauce.

1½oz (40g) fresh ginger, grated
4 tablespoons (60ml) water
1 large Ogen or small honeydew
   melon
4oz (110g) fruit sugar
4 egg yolks
¾ pint (425ml) double cream

2 tablespoons (30ml) lemon juice

Marinade for melon balls
1 dessertspoon (10ml) honey
1 teaspoon (5ml) fresh ginger,
   grated
2 tablespoons (30ml) brandy

To make the ice-cream, soak the grated ginger in the water and leave to stand for 10 minutes. Squeeze out the juice. You should have just about 4fl oz (120ml) of ginger water. Cut off the top of the melon and scoop out the seeds and fibres. If you want to decorate the ice-cream with melon balls, use a small ball scoop to cut out 12 balls from the lid. Set aside to marinate while the ice-cream is chilling (see instructions below for marinade). Spoon out the rest of the melon pulp into a small, thick saucepan. Add the sugar and cook on a low heat until the pulp is soft. Mash with a potato masher, and take off the heat. Whisk the egg yolks until light and cream-coloured. Put the saucepan back on a low heat and, stirring continuously, pour the egg yolks into the melon pulp and then whisk hard until a thin creamy consistency is achieved, then remove from the heat. Let the mixture get cold in the fridge. Whip the cream until it thickens slightly, stir the ginger juice and lemon juice into the cooled pulp, then fold in the cream. Transfer the mixture into a freezer container, cover with a lid and freeze for 2½ hours. Stir the mixture three times during the freezing process.

To marinate the melon balls, melt the honey in a small saucepan, add the grated ginger and stir. Now add the brandy and stir six times over a low heat. Put the melon balls in small bowl and pour over the brandy and ginger sauce. Leave to get cold.

When the ice-cream is well chilled, scoop it into the melon shell or on to a serving dish and decorate with the melon balls. Save the sauce to spoon over individual servings.

Avocado, Orange and Onion Appetiser

Menu 2

Arabian Couscous
Yoghurt Bowl Cooler

Pistachio Pashka
(Chilled curd cheese with glazed fruits)

Avocado, Orange and Onion Appetiser

6 medium oranges, peeled (take off as much pith as possible)
1 medium onion, (approx 5oz (150g) when peeled)
1 medium avocado pear, peeled and de-stoned
3 tablespoons (45ml) olive oil
2 tablespoons (30ml) lemon juice
¼ teaspoon freshly ground black pepper

¼ teaspoon mustard powder
½ level teaspoon clear honey
sea salt to taste, about ½ level teaspoon seems to be about right
rind of 1 orange, very finely grated
bunch of watercress
1 tablespoon (15ml) parsley, very finely chopped

Slice the oranges very thinly on a plate. Pour off the juice and save it. Slice the onion very thinly in rings. Now place the avocado, oil, lemon juice and any orange juice, pepper, mustard, honey, salt and grated orange rind in a liquidiser and blend together for 1 minute. Taste and add little more seasoning or lemon juice if liked.

Arrange the orange slices and onion rings on a serving dish, overlapping each other in circles. Place sprigs of watercress around the edge and one in the centre. Pour on the avocado purée, but do not cover the orange and onion rings completely. Sprinkle a little parsley in a circle 1in (2·5cm) from the central watercress sprig.

Arabian Couscous

You will need to steam the couscous or bulgur for this dish. Couscous is a grain produced from semolina, which is a variety of wheat. Bulgur is described on page 45. In North Africa a special pot called a couscousier is used but a muslin-lined steamer or snug fitting muslin-lined colander placed on top of a deep saucepan will be just as good. The saucepan has to be deep because there is quite a large volume of vegetables to cook.

To prepare the couscous or bulgur
12oz (350g) couscous grain or bulgur wheat (see page 45)
2 tablespoons (30ml) olive oil
¾ pint (350ml) cold water
1 scant teaspoon (4ml) sea salt

Sauce
3 tablespoons (45ml) olive oil
2 medium onions, peeled and coarsely chopped
2 large cloves garlic, crushed
3 medium carrots, scraped and cut in ½in (1cm) slanting ovals

8 oz (225g) potatoes, thinly peeled and coarsely chopped
1 turnip, coarsely chopped
1 large green pepper cut into 1½in (4cm) thickish strips
3 medium size courgettes, quartered lengthwise then cut into 1in (2·5cm) sticks
5oz (150g) dry weight chick peas, cooked (see page 60)
1 generous teaspoon (7ml) ground coriander

1 generous teaspoon (7ml)
  ground cumin
1 generous teaspoon (7ml)
  turmeric
½ teaspoon ground mustard
  seeds
1 scant teaspoon (4ml) chilli
  powder or cayenne pepper

12oz (350g) ripe tomatoes,
  skinned and puréed
1 tablespoon (15ml) tomato purée
4oz (110g) sultanas
¾ pint (425ml) water and 1
  tablespoon (15ml) lemon juice
sea salt to taste
sprigs of mint or parsley

First prepare the couscous. Pour the water, to which you have added the sea salt, over the grains. Drain, then rub the olive oil lightly into the grains to keep them separate. Rub them lightly with your fingertips several times during the next 10 minutes.

To prepare the sauce, heat the oil in a large, thick saucepan. Sauté the onion, garlic, carrot, potato and turnips for 10 minutes, tossing gently to cook them all evenly. Add the peppers and courgettes and continue frying for 3 minutes more. Stir in the cooked chick peas, coriander, cumin, turmeric, ground mustard seeds and chilli powder or cayenne and cook without burning for 1 minute. Add the tomatoes and purée, sultanas, water and lemon juice. Stir well and add salt to taste. Bring to the boil then simmer. Place the soaked couscous in a muslin-lined colander or steamer. Put a lid on top (or foil) and place over the vegetables. Simmer for 30 minutes until the vegetables are soft. When cooked, pour the couscous into a large serving dish and fork in a little oil or butter to keep grains separate. The sauce goes in the cente of the couscous. Decorate with the mint or parsley. Serve with Yoghurt Bowl Cooler (see page 130).

Pistachio Pashka

This dessert originated from Russia. It is a protein-rich sweet which complements a vegetable and grain meal. You will probably only be able to obtain the salted variety of pistachio nuts in shells. Shell these and wash them. Dry in the oven for 5 minutes at 325°F, 160°C, Gas Mark 3 and leave to get cold.

2oz (50g) glacé cherries
2 standard egg yolks
1½oz (40g) fruit sugar
4 tablespoons (60ml) single cream
3oz (75g) butter
1lb (450g) curd cheese
2oz (50g) candied pineapple,
  chopped

2oz (50g) sultanas
2oz (50g) pistachio nuts, chopped
  (use blanched, chopped
  almonds if you like)
3 drops vanilla essence
few sliced pistachio nuts and a few
  glacé cherries to decorate

Wash the cherries and cut in half. Reserve 5 halves for decoration. Beat the egg yolks with the sugar until they are a light cream colour. Bring the single cream to the boil, pour into a jug and then pour over the egg mixture. Return to the saucepan and heat very gently until the mixture thickens, stirring all the time. Leave to cool. Cream the butter and the cheese together. To do this easily, cream a little of the cheese into the butter first, then gradually add the rest of the cheese. Stir in the fruit and the pistachio nuts. Now stir in the cool egg and cream mixture and add the vanilla essence. Line a sieve with muslin and rest it over a bowl. Spoon the pashka mixture into the muslin, flatten the top and fold the ends of the muslin cloth over the top. Put a small plate or saucer on the top plus a weight or stone. The mixture will drip. Put it in the fridge for at least four hours or overnight. Serve sliced.

Menu 3

Leek Timbale
Granary Garlic French Loaf

Stuffed Vegetable Medley
Shades of Green Salad

Carob and Pecan Nut Gateau

Leek Timbale *(illustrated opposite)*

A timbale has an egg custard base with a delicate flavour and very light texture. Traditionally it is made in a dish of the same name which has sloping sides. The timbale is then turned out, much as you would turn out a jelly, and sliced. I prefer to cook and serve the mixture in ramekins. This recipe will fill 6 small ramekins or 4 large size. I have used leeks but a purée of asparagus, spinach or mushrooms is equally delicious.

8oz (225g) leeks (use the white and some of the tenderer parts of the green only. Save the rest for soups)
1 tablespoon (15ml) olive oil or butter
3 tablespoons (45ml) single cream
¼ teaspoon mustard powder
½ teaspoon ground mace

1 scant teaspoon (4ml) tarragon
½ teaspoon sea salt
½ teaspoon freshly ground black pepper
4 standard eggs
3oz (75g) farmhouse Cheddar cheese, grated
8fl oz (225ml) milk

Cut leeks into ½in (1cm) rings. Wash well and dry with kitchen paper. Heat the oil or butter in a pan and sauté the leeks for 10 minutes only. Keep a lid on the pan. Leave to cool. Purée the leeks with the single cream. Put the puréed leeks, spices, tarragon, salt and pepper in a mixing bowl. Whisk the eggs then beat these into the purée. Stir in the cheese. Warm the milk and pour this very gradually into the egg mixture, beating all the time. Grease the ramekins well. Pour the mixture into these filling them not quite to the top. Place the ramekins on a baking tray in which you have put some boiling water. Bake on lowest shelf in the oven at 350°F, 180°C, Gas Mark 4 for 35-40 minutes.

Granary Garlic French Loaf

Makes 2 loaves.

1oz (25g) fresh yeast
1 level teaspoon (5ml) Barbados sugar
¾ pint (425ml) warm water
1lb (450g) granary flour
8oz (225g) 100% strong wholemeal flour, plain
1 generous teaspoon (6ml) sea salt

1 egg yolk
1 tablespoon (15ml) sunflower oil or melted butter
3 good size juicy cloves garlic, crushed
few sesame seeds or cracked wheat for the top

Cream the yeast and sugar and pour in 150ml (just over 5fl oz) of the warm water. Leave to stand, covered with a cloth, in a warm place until

Above left Leek Timbale.

Above right *(top)* Shades of Green Salad (see page 141), *(bottom)* Stuffed Vegetable Medley (see page 140).

frothy, about 7-10 minutes. Mix the flours with the salt. Beat the egg yolk with the oil or melted butter and the crushed garlic. When the yeast liquid is frothy make a well in the flour and pour this in with the egg and garlic mixture and some of the warm water. Mix to a soft dough, adding the remaining water. *(Remember* flours vary, so you might not need so much water. Do not make the dough sticky. When doing any bread recipe it is always best to add the liquid gradually.) Knead for 7 minutes. Place the dough in a greased plastic bag and leave to rise in a warm place until doubled in size. This will take about 1 hour, less if the room is very warm. When well risen knead for 2 more minutes. Divide the dough into two equal parts and roll out each piece to a thick oval 12in (30cm) long and 8in (20cm) wide. Roll the dough over like a swiss roll and press it gently together. This will lighten the dough. Shape the rolled-up dough into a French loaf shape 14in (35cm) long. Place both loaves on a greased baking sheet, leaving room to expand. Slide the baking sheet into a large, greased plastic bag. Leave in a warm place until the loaves are double in size (about 30 minutes).

Pre-heat the oven to 425°F, 220°C, Gas Mark 7. When the loaves are well risen make six slanting indents in each loaf with the back of a knife. Brush the loaves with lukewarm water and sprinkle on cracked wheat or sesame seeds. Bake in the centre of the oven for 15 minutes, turning the tray round after 10 minutes. Turn the loaves upside down and finish the baking for 3 more minutes. Cool on a wire rack.

Stuffed Vegetable Medley *(illustrated on page 139)*

This dish is best during the late summer months when peppers, courgettes and aubergines are in season, more tender and less expensive. The recipe takes quite a bit of preparation but you can cook the rice and sauce filling the day before. Do not combine these until you are ready to fill the vegetables. Use skinned, fresh, soft tomatoes if possible, but if not, canned will do.

Note: *in the ingredients list you will see Holbrooks Sauce. This is a vegetarian equivalent to Worcester Sauce. It is not essential but quite delicious.*

You will need a large baking dish about 14 x 12in (35 x 30cm) or a casserole dish with a lid or foil to cover.

1lb (450g) fresh tomatoes, skinned (canned will do)
3 tablespoons (45ml) olive oil
2 medium onions, peeled and chopped (about 8oz (225g))
2 large juicy cloves garlic, crushed
4oz (110g) button mushrooms
1 teaspoon (5ml) basil
1 bay leaf
1 level teaspoon (5ml) coriander
2 tablespoons (30ml) parsley, chopped
4oz (110g) pine kernels
2 tablespoons (30ml) tomato purée
1 tablespoon (15ml) lemon juice
1 dessertspoon (10ml) Holbrooks Sauce (optional)
sea salt
freshly ground black pepper
8oz (225g) (dry weight) short grain Italian brown rice, cooked (see page 44 for cooking instructions)
4 young red or green peppers (red are sweeter)
2 medium aubergines
4 medium courgettes (about 6in (15cm) long)
a little olive oil for frying

Take out half a teacup of tomato juice from the tomatoes and keep aside. Heat the oil in a frying pan and sauté the onion and garlic for 10 minutes until soft. Add the mushrooms and cook for 3 minutes more. Stir in the basil, bay leaf, coriander, parsley and pine kernels. (Save a few pine kernels and a little parsley to garnish.) Cook for 1 minute only. Now add half the tomato purée, the well mashed tomatoes, lemon and Holbrooks Sauce. Cook for 2 minutes. Taste and add salt and freshly ground black pepper to your liking. The sauce will not be fully cooked as it will have more cooking time in the oven.

Combine the sauce with the cooked rice. Divide the mixture as follows, in three separate dishes: ½ for stuffing the peppers, ¼ for the aubergines, ¼ for the courgettes. Trim both ends off the aubergines. Cut in half lengthwise, sprinkle with salt and leave for 30 minutes.

To stuff the peppers
Cut a slice off the stalk end and pull out the core. Wash out the seeds and wipe the peppers. Place in the baking dish and fill each one with rice mixture.

To stuff the courgettes
Trim both ends, cut in half lengthwise and cut out shallow grooves from each half. Chop the cut-out flesh and sauté in little olive oil for 2 minutes. Mix the flesh with the rice mixture reserved for the courgettes. Fill each long, thin 'boat' and place in the casserole dish with the peppers.

To stuff the aubergines
Rinse the salted aubergines and dry with kitchen paper. Cut out the flesh leaving ½in (1cm) still on the skins. Chop the aubergine pulp into small pieces and sauté in olive oil for a few minutes until soft. Mix with the remaining quarter of the rice mixture. Fill the aubergines with this mixture and place in the baking dish.

To the reserved tomato juice add half a teacup of water and the remaining tomato purée, a little salt and black pepper. Pour this liquid into the baking dish. Cover the dish with foil or a lid. Bake at 350°F, 180°C, Gas Mark 4 for 45 minutes, until the shells of the vegetables are soft. Just before serving sprinkle a few pine kernels and a little chopped parsley on each stuffed vegetable.

Shades of Green Salad *(illustrated on page 139)*

½ good size Chinese leaf or head
   of cos or Webb lettuce
2 bunches fresh green watercress
1 medium size cucumber
2 bunches spring onions, medium
   size

2 tablespoons (30ml) parsley,
   finely chopped
Olive Oil and Lemon Dressing
   (see page 115 for the recipe)
   Use double the amount given
   in the recipe.

Shred the Chinese leaf or lettuce very thinly. Spread this on an oval platter leaving the edge free. Cut off most of the green from the spring onions, leaving 2½in (5·5cm) tops with the bulb and a little green and chop up the green parts very finely. Sprinkle over the lettuce, mixing it well in. Hold the top of each onion and cut through the bulb 6 times to half the length and fan out the shredded top half. Cut the cucumber in thin, lacy rings. Wash the watercress, leaving it in even-size sprigs and taking out any yellow leaves. To arrange your salad, place the sprigs of watercress all round the lettuce and stick in the spring onion tops. They will look like exotic flowers growing out of the watercress. Place the cucumber slices overlapping all round the edge of the plate. Now put one large sprig of watercress in the centre with one spring onion top sticking out of the middle. Circle this with overlapping cucumber slices. Pour over the well-shaken dressing and finally sprinkle over the parsley.

Carob and Pecan Nut Gateau

An electric mixer will give a lighter sponge for this recipe. You will need two 9in (23cm) sandwich tins, greased.

Set the oven to 375°F, 190°C, Gas Mark 5.

Gateau
6oz (175g) polyunsaturated
   margarine
6oz (175g) soft dark sugar
3 eggs, beaten (weight in shells 6oz
   (175g))
6oz (175g) less 1 level tablespoon
   (15ml) 100% wholemeal flour,
   self raising
1 level tablespoon (15ml) carob
   flour

Filling
raspberry jam
Yoghurt Cream (see page 150 for
   recipe) substituting Grand
   Marnier for the apricot brandy
finely grated rind of one medium
   orange
3 drops vanilla essence
2oz (50g) pecan nuts, chopped in
   small pieces (not ground)
1oz (25g) whole pecan nuts for the
   top

Cream the margarine with the sugar until light and fluffy. Add the beaten egg a dessertspoonful at a time. Sift the flour with the carob flour and fold it gradually into the egg mixture. Stir in the orange rind, vanilla essence and chopped pecans. Divide the mixture between the two sandwich tins and bake for 20-25 minutes near the centre of the oven. Change the tins around after 15 minutes. Leave in the tins for 5 minutes before turning out to cool on a wire rack. When cold sandwich together with raspberry jam and a generous helping of the yoghurt cream. Spread a layer of jam on the top of the cake then spread over the rest of the yoghurt cream. Decorate with the pecan nut halves and chill for 30 minutes before serving.

Menu 4

Pistachio Dip with Crudités

Gougère of Asparagus, Mushroom and White Wine
Hot Flageolet Bean Salad
Potatoes Anna

Raspberry Griestorte

Pistachio Dip with Crudités

Dip

2 egg yolks
6fl oz (175ml) olive oil or **sunflower oil**
1 tablespoon (15ml) lemon juice
½ teaspoon mustard powder
½ teaspoon sea salt

½ teaspoon black pepper, freshly ground
1 clove garlic, crushed
1 tablespoon (15ml) fresh parsley, chopped
4oz (110g) pistachio nuts

In a blender grind the nuts to a powder. Take out. Put the egg yolks, 2 tablespoons (30ml) of the olive oil, the lemon juice, mustard, salt, pepper and garlic in a liquidiser and blend at low speed to a smooth paste. Keeping the liquidiser on a low speed, drop in the parsley then pour in the remaining oil in a slow but steady stream. The machine will begin to make a gurgling sound when the mixture starts to thicken. When all the oil is poured in and well blended stop the machine and pour the mayonnaise into a bowl. Grind the nuts to a powder and beat into the mayonnaise. Taste and season with more salt if needed. You can also add a little more lemon juice if you like. Chill.

Crudités (raw vegetables)
A selection of the following vegetables could be used.

1 bunch of spring onions (use only 2½in (7cm) of the bulb end, saving the green tops to use instead of chives in a salad)
3 good size carrots, scraped and cut in ½in (1cm) chunks widthwise then cut into thin sticks (rub with lemon juice to avoid browning)
3 tender (inside) sticks of celery, cut into 2½in (7cm) sticks
½ good size red pepper cut into strips from the centre to the base
½ small cauliflower broken into florets
½ cucumber cut into narrow 2½in (7cm) sticks
Chicory leaves (just break off the leaves which will do nicely as scoops for the sauce)
Long Mediterranean radishes if available (just scrub, trim and dip in whole)

Opposite Gougère with Asparagus, Mushroom and White Wine (see page 144).

To serve put the pistachio dip in a bowl in the centre of a dinner-size plate and arrange the crudités attractively around.

Gougère (choux ring) with Asparagus, Mushroom and White Wine

You can use 100% wholemeal flour for the pastry but I prefer the lightness of 81% wheatmeal. You will need a large pizza tray or ovenproof dish about 11in (28cm) in diameter and a 3in (8cm) metal pastry cutter.

Set the oven to 400°F, 200°C, Gas Mark 6.

(illustrated on page 143)

Choux pastry
5oz (150g) 81% wheatmeal flour, plain, sifted
scant teaspoon (4ml) sea salt
4oz (110g) butter
*¼ pint (142ml) milk
*¼ pint (142ml) water

4 eggs, beaten
4oz (110g) farmhouse Cheddar cheese, grated
¼ teaspoon cayenne pepper

*These amounts must be measured exactly

Add the salt to the sifted flour. Put the butter, milk and water in a large, heavy-based saucepan and cook on a low heat until the butter melts then bring quickly to the boil. Take off the heat and pour in the flour, stirring quickly with a wooden spoon until the flour has absorbed all the liquid. Continue beating until the dough comes away from the sides of the pan. (Do not beat too vigorously.) Leave to cool for 3 minutes. Whisk the eggs with the cayenne and gradually beat into the dough. Finally, beat in the grated cheese. You should have a soft, shiny dough which holds its shape but is not stiff. You can prepare this a few hours in advance, but cover it with greased paper and a saucepan lid to prevent it drying out. Spoon the pastry all around the cutter to the edge of the tin. Take out the cutter, it is only used as a guide. Bake for 45 minutes, until the pastry is well puffed up and golden brown. Do not disturb during cooking or the dough will collapse. When cooked, slit diagonally through the centre with a sharp knife. Keep warm in a low oven until the filling is ready.

Filling
1lb (450g) asparagus, frozen or **fresh (not canned)**
2 tablespoons (30ml) single cream
½ pint (275ml) stock (use vegetable stock cube and hot water if you have no stock)
½ pint (275ml) dry white wine
2oz (50g) butter or **2 tablespoons (30ml) olive oil** or **sunflower oil**
2oz (50g) unbleached white flour

2 tablespoons (30ml) sunflower oil for sautéing vegetables
1 large onion, peeled and finely chopped (approx 8oz (225g))
1 small clove garlic, crushed
12oz (350g) small button mushrooms, wiped and sliced
1 egg yolk
1 scant teaspoon (4ml) lemon peel, finely grated
freshly ground black pepper
sea salt

If using fresh asparagus cut off the hard, woody ends with a sharp knife, and just scrape the whites of the stems. Tie in a bunch, stand the bunch upright, put in a saucepan and pour in boiling salted water to just below the green tips. Boil for 12 minutes. If frozen just steam for 10 minutes. When cooked, cut off the tips (about 1½in (4cm)) and put them carefully on a plate. Chop the stems and purée with the cream. Leave to one side. Heat the stock and wine together and pour into a jug. In a heavy-based saucepan heat the butter or oil. Keep on very low heat. When bubbly add the flour and let it cook for a few minutes, stirring all the time. Gradually pour in the hot stock and wine mixture, stirring with a balloon whisk as you do this. After the sauce thickens continue to cook it for 7 minutes more. Stir often to prevent sticking. Take off the heat and cover with a piece of well-buttered greaseproof paper to stop a skin forming.

In a frying pan sauté the onion and garlic on a low heat for 10 minutes. Take care not to burn the mixture. Keep a lid on the pan. Add the sliced mushrooms and cook for a further 3 minutes. Remove from the heat and add the sautéd vegetables to the white wine sauce. Reheat slowly. Now beat the egg yolk into the asparagus purée with the lemon peel. Take the sauce off the heat and stir in the purée. Season with freshly ground black pepper and a little sea salt if needed. Stir in the asparagus tips with a fork, leaving a few to decorate the top. Take the gougère out of the oven. Take off the top half and spoon on half the filling. Replace the top and spoon the rest of the filling into the centre hole. Decorate with the reserved asparagus tips.

Hot Flageolet Bean Salad *(illustrated on page 62)*

6oz (175g) (dry weight) flageolet beans, cooked and drained (see page 60 on how to cook these beans)

Olive Oil and Lemon Dressing (see page 115 for this recipe)

2 tablespoons (30ml) fresh parsley, chopped, and the chopped green ends of the spring onions if you used these in the crudité recipe

While the beans are still hot toss with the dressing and sprinkle on the parsley and green ends of the spring onions.

Potatoes Anna

You will need a 9in (23cm) baking dish (line the bottom only), greased well, and foil to make a lid.

1½lb (675g) potatoes, (medium size old potatoes are best), scrubbed
sea salt and freshly ground black pepper

polyunsaturated margarine or butter, melted
a little parsley to garnish

Leave the skins on the potatoes. Slice them very thinly and arrange a layer slightly overlapping on the bottom of the dish. Sprinkle on a little sea salt and pepper and pour on a little of the margarine or butter. Continue layering until the potatoes are used up. Press each layer well in. Cover with foil, making sure the foil is right over the rim of the tin and pressed down. Bake at 375°F, 190°C, Gas Mark 5 for 1 hour. Uncover when cooked, turn out on to a serving dish, remove greaseproof paper and garnish with parsley. Slice to serve.

Raspberry Griestorte

Light and delicious for special occasions. You will need a swiss roll tin, 8 x 12in (20 x 30cm), greased and lined and sprinkled with flour and a little soft light sugar. If you have a food processor with a sponge-making attachment this is ideal for the recipe but is not essential.

Set the oven to 350°F, 180°C, Gas Mark 4.

2oz (50g) semolina
1 tablespoon (15ml) ground almonds
3 large eggs, separated
4oz (110g) soft light sugar or 3oz (75g) fruit sugar
grated rind and juice of ½ lemon

Filling
5fl oz (150g) double cream
2 tablespoons (30ml) thick natural yoghurt
1 teaspoon (5ml) clear honey
8oz (225g) raspberries, fresh or frozen

Mix the semolina with the ground almonds. Whisk the egg yolks with the sugar until the mixture is thick and light in colour. Whisk the lemon rind, juice, semolina and almonds into the egg mixture. In another bowl whisk the egg whites until in stiff peaks. Fold in the egg yolk mixture (do not beat, just fold gently). Pour this into the prepared swiss roll tin and level out with a palette knife. Bake for 25-30 minutes. The sponge will be puffed up and pale gold in colour when cooked. Leave for 3 minutes after removing from the oven, then turn out on to a sheet of greaseproof paper on which you've sprinkled a little sugar. Trim the edges of the sponge and roll up with the paper still on. Leave aside to cool. Whisk the cream to a soft, firm consistency and stir in the yoghurt and honey, folding gently together. Unroll the cooled sponge roll – it might crack a little but this won't matter. Peel off the top sheet of greaseproof paper and spread the sponge with the cream mixture, leaving 2 tablespoons (30ml) for decoration. Press the raspberries very gently into the cream, again leaving about 2oz (50g) to decorate. Roll up the griestorte, pressing gently together. Spread the remaining cream on top and decorate with the reserved raspberries.

Menu 5

Marinated Mango and Melon

Oriental Spiced Vegetables with Tofu
Saffron Rice with Toasted Cashews
Japanese Garden Salad

Apricot, Apple and Almond Flan
Yoghurt Cream

Marinated Mango and Melon

This can be eaten before the main dish or as an accompaniment. The flavour blends well with the spicy sauce. You can substitute two ripe peaches for the mango.

1 mango
1 small honeydew melon
1 wineglass of white wine
½ teaspoon ground ginger

½ teaspoon ground cinnamon
1 rounded tablespoon (20ml) soft medium muscovado sugar, sieved

(top left) Oriental Spiced Vegetable with Tofu (see page 148), *(top right)* Saffron Rice with Toasted Cashews (see page 148), *(bottom)* Japanese Garden Salad (page 149).

Wash the mango. Cut the skin as if you are going to cut the fruit into quarters. Peel off each quarter of the skin and with a sharp knife cut thin slices all the way round, easing each one gently off the stone. Place the slices in a dish and cover. Cut the melon in half lengthwise, scoop out the seeds and fibres and cut each half in two lengthwise. With a sharp knife cut off the skin from each piece and cube the flesh. Place the melon flesh in the dish with the mango slices. Stir the ginger, cinnamon and sugar into the wine and melt over a low heat — do not allow to boil. Pour over the fruit. Chill for 30 minutes before serving.

Oriental Spiced Vegetables with Tofu *(illustrated on page 147)*

It is important to have a firm pressed tofu for this delicately spiced recipe. See page 80 for how to make this. You can substitute 12oz (350g) (cooked weight) black eye beans for the tofu if you wish (see page 57 for how to cook these). You will need an ovenproof casserole dish.

1 teaspoon (5ml) sea salt
2 tablespoons (30ml) lemon juice
curl of lemon peel
1 bay leaf
1 cinnamon stick
5oz (150g) onion, peeled and cut into thin rings (weight after peeling)
5oz (150g) red and green peppers, coarsely chopped
4oz (110g) small button mushrooms, wiped and sliced
½ pint (275ml) boiling water
2 tablespoons (30ml) sesame seed oil or olive oil
1 slightly rounded tablespoon (20ml) 100% wholemeal flour, plain

1 teaspoon (5ml) methi (fenugreek leaf)
1 level teaspoon (4ml) coriander, ground
1 slightly rounded dessertspoon (10ml) medium curry powder
12oz (350g) ripe tomatoes, skinned and chopped, (tinned tomatoes can be used)
1lb (450g) firm tofu
2 tablespoons (30ml) shoyu (naturally fermented soy sauce)
oil for shallow frying, plus a small amount of 100% wholewheat flour for coating the tofu

Put the salt, lemon juice, lemon curl, bay leaf, cinnamon stick, onion rings, peppers and mushrooms into the boiling water and cook for 5 minutes only. Remove from the heat. Heat the oil in a frying pan, stir in the flour, methi, and coriander and curry powder and cook on a low heat for 2 minutes only. *Do not burn the mixture.* Take off the heat. Drain the vegetables, remove the bay leaf and cinnamon stick and place the vegetables in a casserole dish. Pour the liquid into a jug. Gradually stir the hot stock into the curry and flour mixture until a smooth sauce. Leave it to cool for 3 minutes then add the chopped tomatoes. Cook for 3 more minutes. Strain the sauce through a sieve, squashing with a wooden spoon to get as much through as possible. The sauce will be a rich, warm brown, smooth and not too thick. Take out one teacupful and reserve. Pour the rest of the sauce over the vegetables in the casserole dish. Cover the dish and place it on the bottom shelf of the oven on lowest heat to keep warm.

Ten minutes before serving, cut the tofu into 1in (2·5cm) cubes. Sprinkle with shoyu. Dip in the flour and shallow fry in the oil, turning to brown all sides until golden in colour. (You can deep-fry this if you wish.) Heat the reserved teacup of spiced sauce. Fork the tofu gently into the vegetables in the casserole and pour over the remaining spiced sauce. Serve within 10 minutes.

Saffron Rice with Toasted Cashews *(illustrated on page 147)*

Try to get Surinam rice as this is the quickest-cooking brown rice.

12oz (350g) Surinam long grain brown rice
1 good pinch saffron or 1 level teaspoon (4ml) turmeric
1 teaspoon (5ml) sea salt
2 tablespoons (30ml) sunflower or olive oil

1 large onion, peeled and chopped
1 small clove garlic, crushed
4oz (110g) cashew nuts
1 tablespoon (15ml) lemon juice
1 tablespoon (15ml) shoyu (naturally fermented soy sauce)
little chopped parsley to garnish

Wash the rice carefully in a sieve. You will have about two cups of rice. Add just under four cups of water, the saffron or turmeric and the sea salt and bring to the boil. Turn down to simmer, put a tight lid on and leave to cook for 25 minutes. Drain if necessary and spread the rice on a baking sheet to cool. Sauté the onion and garlic in the oil until light golden brown. Take care not to burn the mixture. Stir in the rice and fry gently for 1 minute. Now put the cashew nuts in a clean dry pan and toast on a low heat, stirring constantly, until golden brown. Take off the heat. Add the lemon juice and shoyu to the rice and fork in the cashew nuts, saving some of the nuts to decorate the top. Put the rice mixture into a serving bowl, sprinkle with the remaining nuts and a little parsley to garnish.

Japanese Garden Salad *(illustrated on page 147)*

This is a simple salad, but it looks very beautiful.

1 lettuce with a good heart
1 bunch watercress
1 bunch radishes

Dressing
6 tablespoons (90ml) sesame seed or
  safflower seed oil
2 tablespoons (30ml) wine vinegar

1 tablespoon (15ml) shoyu
  (naturally fermented soy sauce)
1 scant teaspoon (4ml) clear honey
½ level teaspoon dry mustard
½ level teaspoon freshly ground
  black pepper
1 good size clove garlic, crushed

Wash and trim the lettuce and watercress. Dry in kitchen paper and put in the refrigerator until time to assemble the salad. To make radishes into flower-like shapes, top and tail and make six cuts lengthwise from the base towards the stalk end with a sharp knife, leaving the last $\frac{1}{8}$in (0·5cm) uncut. Place the radishes in a bowl of iced water and they will open like flowers.

Make the dressing by putting all the ingredients into a screw-top jar. Shake well just before use.

To assemble the salad, place the lettuce leaves on a round or oval plate. Put sprigs of watercress on top, pushing the stalk ends into the lettuce, and arrange the radish 'flowers' around the watercress. Cover with a plastic sheet or clingfilm and place in the fridge until time to serve. Pour over the dressing just before serving.

Apricot, Apple and Almond Flan *(illustrated on page 26)*

The method used here for pastry-making releases the gluten (protein) in the flour and lightens the pastry considerably. You will need a 9in (23cm) loose-bottomed flan tin, well greased.

4oz (110g) polyunsaturated margarine
1 level tablespoon (15ml) soft light muscovado sugar
1 egg yolk
2 tablespoons (30ml) cold water
pinch sea salt

4oz (110g) 100% wholemeal flour, plain
4oz (110g) 81% extraction flour, plain
1 scant teaspoon (4ml) baking powder

Cream the margarine and sugar for 1 minute. Whisk the egg yolk with the water. Mix all the dry ingredients together. Add the egg and water with 2 tablespoons (30ml) of the flour mixture, using a wooden spoon, until the dough is thick. Add the last bits of the flour with your hands. Knead the dough for 2 minutes (this is very important). Place in a plastic bag and refrigerate for 30 minutes or put in the freezer for 10-15 minutes.

Roll out the dough on a lightly-floured surface. Slide a palette knife under the dough, lift an edge on to your rolling pin and curl the pastry around it. Roll this on to the prepared flan tin and prick the base. Chill in the freezer or refrigerator for 5 minutes more. Bake blind at 375°F, 190°C, Gas Mark 5, for 10 minutes.

Filling

4oz (110g) dried apricots, washed and soaked overnight in ¾ pint (425ml) water plus 1 tablespoon (15ml) clear honey
1 large cooking apple, peeled, cored and chopped
2oz (50g) ground almonds

1 level teaspoon (5ml) cinnamon
¼ teaspoon clove powder
2 tablespoons (30ml) clear honey
1 medium size cooking apple, (leave whole)
1 tablespoon (15ml) apple juice concentrate

Liquidise the soaked apricots with the juice and the chopped cooking apple. Stir in the ground almonds, cinnamon, clove powder and 1 tablespoon (15ml) of the honey. Spread this mixture on the base of the cooked pastry case. Cut the whole cooking apple into quarters (leave skin on). Core and then slice each section into very thin wedges. Overlap these all around the edge of the flan. Make another circle in the middle. Heat the remaining honey with the apple juice concentrate and pour over the apples. Bake at 375°F, 190°C, Gas Mark 5, for 20-30 minutes until the apples are soft on top.

Yoghurt Cream

10oz (275g) natural yoghurt
5oz (150g) double cream
1 teaspoon (5ml) honey

1 dessertspoon (10ml) apricot brandy (optional)

Tie the yoghurt in a piece of muslin or thin cotton cloth and leave to drip for 3 hours. You will end up with a thick, smooth yoghurt cheese. The longer you leave it to drip the thicker the cheese. Whisk the double cream until thick and whisk in the yoghurt cheese. Stir in the honey and liqueur.

Buffet Party Menu

Garlic (or Granary Garlic) French Loaves

Wholemeal Pizzas
Asparagus (or Leek*) Quiche with Tarragon
Spinach, Cottage Cheese and Yoghurt Quiche

Pierogi*
Curried Rice and Chick Pea Balls

Saffron Rice with Almonds and Sweetcorn*
Bulgur Salad (Lebanese style)
Bean Sprout Salad with Mushrooms
Red Cabbage Salad with Pecan Nuts

Nutty Paté
Marrowfat Pea and Chilli Dip*
Hummous
Crudites

Peach Chutney   Green Tomato Chutney

Apricot Brandy and Mango Trifle*
Carob and Pecan Nut Gateau
Fresh Fruit Salad*

The quantities given in this chapter are sufficient for about thirty guests. You will be familiar with most of the recipes already (those marked * are new in this section), but I have included advice on cooking ahead and freezing/refrigerating of recipes which appear elsewhere in the book, plus any ingredient changes necessary to cater for the larger numbers involved. It is useful to be able to prepare foods in advance when giving a buffet party, then all you have to do on the day of the party is to add the finishing touches. Doing it this way avoids panic and the problem of having a thousand unwashed dishes piled up in the kitchen an hour before your guests arrive!

Garlic French Loaves or Granary Garlic French Loaves

(See pages 16 and 138 for recipes.)

Makes 6.

When baked, allow the loaves to cool on a wire rack, then wrap each in foil and put the lot into a large plastic bag. Tie and freeze. To defrost, take the loaves out of the plastic bag and lay them out, still in their foil wrappers, to defrost completely. This will take about an hour. Once defrosted, take them out of the foil, brush with a little warm, very slightly salted water and put in the oven at 375°F, 190°C, Gas Mark 5 for 7 minutes just before serving.

Wholemeal Pizzas

(See page 14 for the recipe.)

Makes 2 large pizzas.

Make up only half the amount of dough given in the recipe, that is, use only 1½lb (750g) wholemeal flour and ¾oz (37g) dried yeast. Halve everything else in the recipe. If you intend to freeze the pizzas, line the base of the tins with a circle of greaseproof paper before baking. Cook the pizzas for 20 minutes only. Do not allow to brown. Remove the pizzas from the oven and allow to get cold then wrap in foil and put each into a plastic bag and freeze. To defrost, remove from the freezer, leave for 10 minutes then unwrap carefully. Do not pull the foil off – wait until it peels off easily. Leave the unwrapped pizzas to defrost completely (this will take about 2 hours) then bake at 375°F, 190°C, Gas Mark 5 for 15 minutes. Serve hot or cold.

Quiches

It is best to prepare only the pastry cases in advance for these. Filling with fresh ingredients gives a much nicer flavour and texture. Make the pastry (see page 18) using 1lb (450g) flour, etc. Line two 9-10in (23-25cm) flan tins with the pastry, put into large plastic bags, squeezing out all the air, and freeze. When you are ready to make the quiches, remove from the freezer and leave to thaw slightly for 15 minutes, then bake blind at 375°F, 190°C, Gas Mark 5 for 10 minutes only.

The **Asparagus Quiche** recipe is given on page 20 and the **Spinach Quiche** recipe on page 21.

Leek Quiche with Tarragon

As an alternative to asparagus, this leek filling is simple and delicious.

All you do is substitute 3 medium leeks for the asparagus and omit the onion. Slice the leeks into ½in (0·6cm) rings, using all the white and only a little of the paler green parts. Wash and pat dry. Sauté in a little olive oil on a low heat for 10 minutes with the lid on. Leave to cool slightly then spoon into the baked quiche case and continue as for Asparagus Quiche. Well worth trying.

Pierogi

Originally from Poland, these are miniature pasties made from a rich cheese pastry and filled with mushrooms and sour cream. Make the pasties and the filling the day before, fill them on the afternoon of the party and bake when ready to eat. They are delicious hot or cold. To reheat just put in a low oven for 10 minutes.

Makes 30.

Pastry
8oz (225g) polyunsaturated margarine
4oz (110g) cream cheese
1 egg, beaten
1lb (450g) 81% wheatmeal flour
1 level teaspoon (5ml) sea salt
egg for glazing and sealing edges of pasties

Filling
3 tablespoons (45ml) olive oil
1lb (450g) small button mushrooms, washed, well dried and finely chopped
1 large onion, very finely chopped (about 8oz (225g))
3 slices wholemeal bread (see page 13) soaked in little white wine
2 eggs, hard-boiled
1 teaspoon (5ml) marjoram
4 tablespoons (60ml) sour cream or thick natural yoghurt
sea salt and plenty of freshly ground black pepper to taste

First make the pastry. Cream the margarine and cheese together, add the beaten egg with 1 tablespoon (15ml) of the flour, and cream it in. Sieve the remaining flour with the salt and gradually add to the creamed mixture. Form into a soft dough, place in a plastic bag and refrigerate overnight. If you do not wish to leave the pastry overnight, it can be used after 1 hour in the fridge.

To make the filling, sauté the onion in olive oil with a lid on until soft, add the mushrooms and the marjoram and sauté for another 2 minutes. Remove from the heat. Mash the soaked bread with a potato masher and stir into the mushrooms. Sieve the hard-boiled eggs and add the sour cream, sea salt and black pepper. Allow to cool before filling the pasties. Store in the refrigerator if the filling is made in advance.

When you are ready to make the pasties, set the oven to 375°F, 190°C, Gas Mark 5. Roll out the dough on a well-floured surface (place a plastic sheet over the dough as you roll – this helps to stop it sticking and prevents the addition of too much flour which can dry out this delicious pastry). Roll the pastry to ⅛in (0·3cm) thick. Using a plain-edge pastry cutter 3in (8cm) in diameter, cut out 30 circles. Place a heaped teaspoon (10ml) of the filling in the centre of each circle. Egg-brush the edges, *fold up* to the centre and press gently together. Brush the tops with egg and bake for about 15 minutes until golden brown.

Curried Rice and Chick Pea Balls

Make up the recipe (see page 48). When the rice mixture is cold, squash together but do not make into balls. Put in a double plastic bag, tie well and freeze.

To make the balls, let the mixture defrost completely overnight, still in the bag. When completely defrosted, form into small balls a little smaller than the recipe states (you should be able to get 30 out of this amount of mixture). Deep fry as instructed. These are nice hot or cold.

Saffron Rice with Almonds and Sweetcorn

1 large onion, peeled and finely
    chopped
1 clove garlic, crushed
2 tablespoons (30ml) corn or
    sunflower oil
8oz (225g) long grain brown rice
1 pint (550ml) hot stock or
    1 vegetable stock cube dissolved
     in water
pinch saffron or a little turmeric

4oz (110g) frozen peas
4oz (110g) frozen sweetcorn
4oz (110g) almonds, blanched and
    split
½ teacup Sweet and Sour Dressing
    (see page 114)
2 tablespoons (30ml) fresh
    parsley, chopped, to garnish
few toasted almonds to garnish

Fry the onion and garlic in the oil for 10 minutes. Add the washed and drained rice and stir with the onions until lightly coloured (about 4 minutes). Add the stock and saffron or turmeric. Bring to the boil, cover and simmer for 25-30 minutes. Cook the peas and sweetcorn in a little boiling salted water for 5 minutes only. Toast the almonds in the oven for 10 minutes. Add the almonds and peas to the rice, forking in gently. Leave to cook, then pour over the Sweet and Sour Dressing and fork this in gently. Place the salad in a serving bowl, and garnish with parsley and a few toasted almonds.

This recipe can be made the day before. Let the mixture get cold, cover and refrigerate then add the dressing half an hour before the party.

Bulgur Salad (Lebanese style)

(See page 53 for the recipe.)

Another grain salad which is always popular. Serve piled on a flattish dish, surrounded by fresh, crisp lettuce leaves. Decorate with sprigs of watercress and parsley. This dish is improved by being made the day before. The flavours merge beautifully overnight.

The recipe for **Bean Sprout Salad with Mushrooms** is given on page 109 and **Red Cabbage Salad with Pecan Nuts** on page 110.

Nutty Paté

(See page 94 for the recipe.)

To make in advance, toast the nuts, liquidise them and put the lot in the freezer to retain their delicious flavour. Defrost completely by placing in a bowl and letting them stand for 1 hour. Break them up as they defrost. This speeds up the process. Add the remaining ingredients and mix well together to serve.

Marrowfat Pea and Chilli Dip

This dip is quite delicious and fiery in taste. (You can use green split peas which do not need soaking. Cook these for 40 minutes.)

8oz (225g) marrowfat peas (dry weight)
6 small green chillies or 1 rounded teaspoon (7ml) chilli powder
1½ pints (825ml) cold water
1 teaspoon (5ml) fresh ginger root, finely grated
1 cinnamon stick

3 tablespoons (45ml) fresh lime juice or lemon juice
1 teaspoon (5ml) aniseed, ground with a pestle and mortar
½ teaspoon freshly ground black pepper
sea salt to taste
cucumber slices to decorate

Soak the peas overnight. Change the water 2 or 3 times. Rinse the peas. Chop the chillies. Liquidise them (or the chilli powder) with the water, ginger and cinnamon stick. Put the chilli water in a saucepan with the peas, bring to the boil and cook till soft (about 1¼ hours). Drain the peas and reserve 4 tablespoons (60ml) of the cooking water. Put the peas, the reserved cooking water, lime juice, ground aniseed and pepper in the liquidiser and blend to a smooth purée. Taste and add sea salt to taste. Place the mixture in a serving bowl, decorating the edge with thinly-sliced cucumber.

You can freeze this dip when cold. Defrost overnight.

Note: Some chillies are not hot. Cut one, lick your finger and press it on the cut chilli. Lick your finger again and you will soon find out if you have hot chillies! Hot ones are need for this recipe.

Hummous

Add a level tablespoon (15ml) of finely chopped fresh mint to the recipe given on page 128 and a little sprig of mint in the centre of the dip to garnish. You can use haricot or soya beans instead of chick peas if you wish. The dip can be frozen when cold. Defrost overnight.

Ideas for **Crudités** to serve with the dips are to be found on page 142.

Now to the sweet dishes. No buffet is complete without a trifle. Here is a recipe for a large and slightly different, rather rich one. As it's not possible to buy wholemeal sponge cake it is best to make the very simple Victoria Sandwich recipe (see page 33). This can be made in advance and frozen. It will defrost in 3 hours.

Apricot Brandy and Mango Trifle

1½ pints (825ml) milk
5 large eggs
5oz (150g) fruit sugar
4 drops vanilla essence
¼ teaspoon nutmeg
1½ lb (675g) fresh apricots
1 good size mango

12oz (350g) wholemeal sponge cake
4 tablespoons (60ml) apricot brandy
double cream for top (approx ½ pint (275ml))

First make the custard. Heat the milk (do not allow to boil) to blood temperature. Beat the eggs with 2oz (50g) of the fruit sugar. Pour on the warm milk, stirring all the time and add the vanilla essence and nutmeg. Pour the custard into a double boiler or into a pan over hot but not boiling water and cook on a low heat until the sauce thickens and the custard coats the back of the spoon. Cover with a damp piece of greaseproof paper and leave to stand while you prepare the fruit.

Wash the apricots, cut in half and remove the stones. Slit the mango skins as if cutting in four and peel off the skin. Slice pieces of fruit off the stone. Put the apricots and mango in a saucepan with the remaining fruit sugar and 6 tablespoons (90ml) water. Cook until soft over a low heat. (Take out 4 apricot halves when only half cooked to use for decoration). Set aside to cool. When cool, place in a trifle serving bowl and crumble the sponge cake over this. Pour on the brandy and break up with a fork so that the crumbs absorb the liquids. Spoon on the custard. Leave to set in the fridge for about 2½ hours. Just before serving whip the cream until stiff and pipe over the top. Decorate with thin slices of apricot.

The recipe for **Carob and Pecan Nut Gateau** can be found on page 138.

Fresh Fruit Salad

Offering a fruit salad is a must. Use plenty of soft fruit like fresh, lightly cooked and cooled apricots or ripe sliced peaches to help the salad juices. Chop all the fruit finely. Halve grapes and de-seed. Leave skins on apples and add toasted chopped almonds or hazel-nuts. Sprinkle lemon juice on apples, pears and bananas to stop them going brown. Add the juices of fresh orange and lemon and little white wine and you can't go wrong.

Afterword

I sincerely hope that these lessons have helped my readers to enjoy wholefoods and encouraged them to experiment with Nature's whole goodness. The most important thing to remember is that food should always be both tasty and healthy. Variations, with or without meat, are endless.

I also hope that the book will enable you to avoid the failures which can so easily discourage the use of unfamiliar foods. Just get your imagination going once you have mastered the basic cooking methods of these worthy ingredients and you will gain so much more than just a tasty meal.

Acknowledgements

I would like to express my grateful thanks to the following people for their assistance in the preparation of this book:
Clive Bowen of Shebbear Pottery, near Beaford, Devon, who kindly loaned some of his pottery; Richard Champion of Yeo Vale Pottery, Yeo Vale, near Bideford, Devon who not only generously loaned items of his stoneware, but also kindly allowed the food photography to be done at his home; also to Eric Birchell, Annabelle Brown, Pam Canavan, Rachel Champion and Deanne Derry.

I would also like to say thank you to Ken Seymour of Television South West who gave me the opportunity to demonstrate some of my recipes in a short TV series.

Nigari and tofu presses are available by post from:

Pauls Tofu,
The Old Brewery,
Wheathampstead House,
Wheathampstead,
St. Albans,
Herts.

Telephone: 058 283 4241

Index